CRAFTING A
PATTERNED
HOME

ALSO BY KRISTIN NICHOLAS

Colorful Stitchery:
65 Embroidery Projects to Personalize Your Home

Crafting a Colorful Home:
A Room-by-Room Guide to Personalizing Your Space with Color

CRAFTING A
PATTERNED
HOME

PAINTING, PRINTING, AND STITCHING PROJECTS TO ENLIVEN EVERY ROOM

KRISTIN NICHOLAS

Photographs by Rikki Snyder

R

Roost Books

BOULDER

2018

Roost Books
An imprint of Shambhala Publications, Inc.
4720 Walnut Street
Boulder, Colorado 80301
roostbooks.com

9 8 7 6 5 4 3 2 1

First Edition
Printed in China

⊗ This edition is printed on acid-free paper that meets the
American National Standards Institute Z39.48 Standard.
♻ Shambhala Publications makes every effort to print
on recycled paper. For more information please visit
www.shambhala.com.

Distributed in the United States by Penguin Random House
LLC and in Canada by Random House of Canada Ltd

BOOK AND COVER DESIGN BY SHUBHANI SARKAR

Library of Congress Cataloging-in-Publication Data

Names: Nicholas, Kristin, author. | Snyder, Rikki, photogra-
    pher (expression)
Title: Crafting a patterned home: painting, printing, and
    stitching projects to enliven every room / Kristin Nicholas;
    photographs by Rikki Snyder.
Description: First edition. | Boulder, Colorado: Roost Books,
    an imprint of Shambhala Publications, Inc., [2018]
Identifiers: LCCN 2017008660 | ISBN 9781611803495 (hard-
    cover: alk. paper)
Subjects: LCSH: Handicraft. | House furnishings.
Classification: LCC TT857 .N515 2018 | DDC 745.5—dc23
LC record available at https://lccn.loc.gov/2017008660

FOR MY SISTERS:

LYNN, LAURIE, NANCY, AND JENNIFER

"TELL ME AND
I'LL FORGET IT.

SHOW ME AND
I MAY REMEMBER.

INVOLVE ME AND
I LEARN."

—BENJAMIN FRANKLIN

CONTENTS

PART ONE
INDOOR SPACES

CHAPTER ONE
KITCHEN AND DINING ROOM

CHAPTER TWO
LIVING ROOM AND LIBRARY

CHAPTER THREE
BATHROOM AND BEDROOM

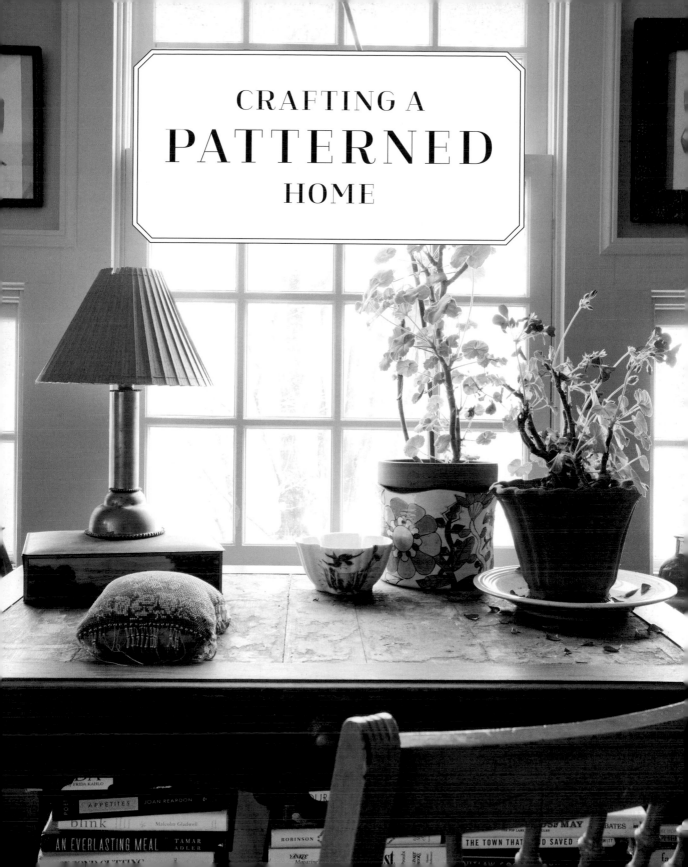

CRAFTING A
PATTERNED
HOME

INTRODUCTION

Pattern is inspiring and intoxicating. It is warm and welcoming. It is cheerful and full of joy. It is exotic and worldly. Pattern is also everywhere we look. Our lives are filled with pattern—on our clothing; on the floors we walk on; on notebooks, labels, and stationery; and on packaging at the grocery store. Pattern is omnipresent in our lives.

I have been interested in pattern since I was a child. I can remember being fascinated with the wallpaper in my bedroom. As I was trying to fall asleep, I would search for the point the floral pattern began again. It's a funny thing to remember, but it is such a deep memory. From those dreamy beginnings, I have been involved with textiles all my life. I have picked up my pattern-making skills along the way. Observation has been the best teacher. By looking at a lot of things—fabrics, wallpapers, interior design magazines—and by visiting museums, historic homes, and contemporary art and craft shows, I have seen how others use pattern. Travel has also informed my use of pattern. In Portugal, I fell in love with the patterned tiles that dotted every street corner, building, and church from floor to ceiling. In London and Paris, I lusted after the patterned designs in the subways and museums. In Venice, the marble floors blew away my pattern-crazy mind.

Clearly, I am not alone in my love of pattern. Throughout the world, pattern plays an enormous part in the decoration of homes, buildings, churches, and temples and on the fabrics of the clothes we wear. Visit every country in the world and you will learn about their individual traditions and styles of patterns. A closer look at these designs will reveal that most of the patterns were made by hand in the past. It is only since the Industrial Revolution of the late 1800s that patterns began to be made by machine.

Handmade pattern has a quality to it that cannot be obtained by any machine. Although repetitive and perhaps monotonous, making patterns by hand is at the same time challenging and creative. Patterns that are made by hand have subtle variances in color, shading, and spacing that give a more interesting, alive, and beautiful look than any machine-patterned object. The slight variations in a hand-printed textile or hand-painted wall, the uneven tension on a hand-knit pillow, the different-size stitches on a hand-embroidered dishtowel all give the patterned

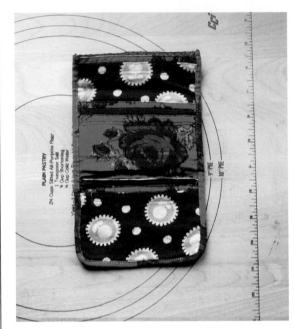

object more authenticity. Although most of the patterned things you use every day were probably made by a machine, the good news is that making patterns by hand is not hard to do. With a few simple tools and some easy-to-learn skills, you can fill your home and life with handmade pattern.

In this book, I will share with you how I have decorated my home with colorful patterns. On the walls, on furniture, on ceramics, on tables, picnic baskets, and more—no surface is safe from my pattern-obsessed mind. With brushes, paint, needles and threads, glue, foam stamps, cardboard, and a little imagination, I have transformed our farmhouse into a pattern-filled world. I'm here to share with you how you too can bring a little (or a lot) of pattern into your home and life.

If these crafts are new to you or if you're feeling overwhelmed, start with a small project such

as a stitched dishtowel or a printed napkin. Look for an already patterned fabric and add more pattern to it with paint or stitches. Build up your confidence by combining different patterns. Then move on to larger projects in your home. An old piece of furniture might beg to be transformed. A wall in your dining room or bedroom might benefit from a hand-painted mural. There is no need to be an experienced artist. Most of the techniques I've included in this book are actually quite easy for the novice.

As you add patterns to your home, you will feel more confident combining designs. Remember that any new skill takes practice before you become proficient. And if at first you feel like you failed, just add some more pattern! Work up your nerve, gather your supplies—you will find you already have many of them in your home. And then begin.

EXPLORING PATTERNS

A pattern is simply a repeated decorative design. Patterns can be textured, printed, woven, knit, crocheted, embroidered, and painted. Pattern is all around us. Look around the space you are in now for patterns—most likely you'll find patterns on the floor, on the walls, on the ceiling, on your clothing, and on the chair where you're sitting. Patterns can be simple or extremely complex, and they offer a world of possibilities to the maker. Let's look at the different types of patterns that make up the decorative landscape. They include geometric patterns, organic patterns, and figurative patterns.

GEOMETRIC PATTERNS

Geometric patterns feature repeating individual geometric shapes or combinations of shapes. They are simple to make by hand and offer an incredible range of combinations and possibilities. They are often referred to as graphic designs.

DOTS AND SPOTS

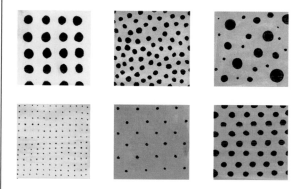

One of the most basic of all patterns is the simple dot. Dots offer all kinds of design potential. They can be big or small. They can be spaced evenly or unevenly across a surface. They can be one size or in many sizes. Most likely, one of the first designs you ever drew as a toddler was a picture covered with dots. We find dots in nature—the sun and full moon, rocks, oranges and fruits, specks of sand or salt, peas, seeds, and more. In the world of surface design, polka dots are a classic dot pattern. They fade in and out of fashion, but for me, they will always be a design that adds a graphic, happy quality to any room.

STRIPES

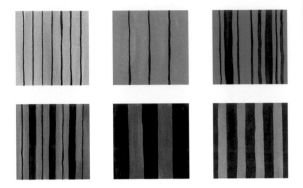

After dots, the next simplest and most basic geometric pattern is a stripe. Begin with a solid-colored fabric or ground and add a straight line of color and then another. (A *ground* is a design term for the background of a pattern. It can refer to paper, fabric, and 3-D objects.) The repetition of the straight line becomes a pattern that we call "stripes." Stripes can be very thin (pencil stripes) or very thick (awning stripes). Stripes can be repeated across a fabric or room spaced equally (called "even stripes") or in unequal spacing and width (called "uneven stripes"). Repeating any line and spacing makes a pattern.

CHECKS AND PLAIDS

All patterns are building blocks to other patterns. By repeating an element and adding to or varying the design element, a different pattern will emerge. Begin with a basic stripe design, turn it 90 degrees on top of itself, and a check or plaid is formed. Alter the thickness and the order of the stripes to form different patterns. There are literally millions of possible combinations. Plaids and checks can be woven, printed by machine, or painted by hand.

DIAGONALS AND ZIGZAGS

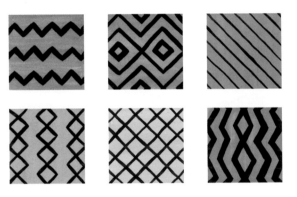

A simple stripe turned on a 45-degree slant makes a diagonal pattern. Cut the diagonal stripe in half and flip one-half of the pattern 90 degrees to make a chevron. Repeat the chevron across a ground and it makes a zigzag design. Vary the length and width of each zigzag and more patterns will emerge. Create mirror images and a different zigzag pattern will emerge.

GEOMETRIC SHAPES

I was a total failure at geometry. I just could not grasp the principles at all. On the other hand, give me a geometric shape and I can make a beautiful surface pattern. Perhaps it was my early introduction to quilting and piecework that made me comfortable with geometric designs. Any geometric shape can be used in a pattern. I like to use the following geometric shapes to build patterns:

- circles
- ovals
- triangles
- squares
- rectangles
- hexagons
- diamonds

The combinations are endless. Geometric elements can be evenly spaced, scattered, layered, and more. Pair one shape with another, and a different pattern will emerge. Sometimes I doodle a geometric pattern on a paper napkin when I am out and about. It is amazing what fun patterns will emerge when you let your mind and pen wander. Frequently I use Adobe Illustrator to design geometric patterns because of its repeat and spacing functions. Once I plan the design on my computer, I will execute it by hand through printing, stamping, knitting, crochet, or embroidery. It will then have an honest, handmade quality to it. The computer is a great tool and a means to the handmade ends.

ORGANIC PATTERNS

Although I do love simple patterns and those made up of geometric shapes, my favorite designs to paint and create are organic in nature. Floral, curvy, natural, relaxed, fluid, and irregular—I find I gravitate toward building handmade patterns based on the plants, vines, leaves, and flowers I see outside my kitchen door. Organic inspiration is all around you, wherever you look. If you lack the time to wander outside to gather natural materials, find images online to fuel your organic design ideas.

I am not the most precise person. The freedom to be a little more creative and less focused on geometric precision when drawing and hand-making organic shapes is more appealing to me. These are some of my favorite organic motifs:

- flowers and fruits
- leaves, stems, buds, roots
- vines
- hearts and swirls
- Tree of Life
- paisleys

FIGURATIVE PATTERNS

The last type of design that is often used in making patterns is figurative representations of animals and things. Figurative designs require a bit more drawing and painting skills to incorporate them in a handmade pattern design. Figurative patterns include the following:

- animals—chickens, sheep, dogs, cats, lions, tigers, elephants, and more
- people and places—pastoral scenes with people, animals, trees, and flowers (for example, the Toile de Jouy design and fabric that originated in the 1700s in France)

- teapots, teacups, vases, and other domestic items
- holiday-themed illustrations, such as Christmas and Halloween motifs

PATTERN REPEATS

Now that you know where to look and what motifs to use for pattern design, let's look at how they can be put to use in a repeat.

STRAIGHT REPEAT

A straight repeat is completely symmetrical. The same motif will be spaced next to, above, and below one another, producing a design that follows a grid. When making a straight repeat by hand, it is helpful to use a physical guide, such as a piece of cardboard or a ruler, to make the spacing more precise.

HALF DROP REPEAT

A half drop repeat moves every other vertical column of motifs halfway down, creating a shift in the pattern. A physical guide is helpful with the initial spacing of this type of repeat. Once the pattern is established, it is easy to eyeball it.

BRICK REPEAT

A brick repeat (sometimes called a half brick repeat) is similar to a half drop repeat, but instead of dropping vertically, the motif is moved horizontally halfway across to create a shift. It gets its name from the way the bricks are laid. Like with a half drop repeat, a physical guide is helpful with the initial spacing, but once the pattern is established, it can often be eyeballed.

RANDOM REPEAT

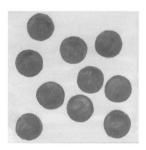

A random repeat occurs when motifs are printed with unequal spacing over the surface of an object. When printing or painting patterns by hand, a random repeat is the easiest because it is the least precise.

OTHER PATTERN DESIGN CONCEPTS

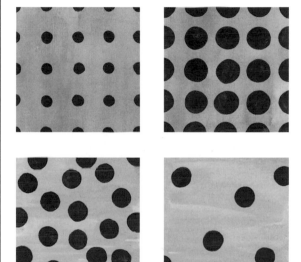

Once you learn the basic ways to make a repeat, you can alter them to create other forms of patterns.

SCALE

Any motif can be made larger or smaller to create a different effect. In the design world, this effect is often referred to as the scale of a motif. Different scale motifs can also be combined within one pattern.

SPACING

In pattern design, the spacing between motifs is generally equal across a pattern. The exception to this is with random repeats. Motifs can be very close to each other or spaced far apart depending upon the desired outcome. If motifs are spaced closely, the pattern will appear more solid from far away and the motifs will be indistinguishable except when viewing up close. If motifs are spaced far apart, a pattern will feel lighter and more open because more of the background is visible.

BORDERS

Any repeat can be used in a single line to create a border or edge of a pattern. Border patterns are also combined with other patterns such as a border of a wallpaper design or the edge of a skirt.

MAKING PATTERNS

There are many ways to design a pattern. You can draw it by hand with pencil and paper. You can use a computer to design it with a drawing or painting program. You can paint it with a paintbrush. Here are some ways to start creating the motifs that you can build patterns around.

DRAWING MOTIFS

Precision is the key when making geometric patterns. My basic tool for drawing simple geometric patterns is a see-through quilting ruler with gridded lines. I use it to draw squares, rectangles, and triangles. I also use lids of jars, glasses, and other vessels to trace circle motifs. Platters often are oval shaped and are perfect templates to trace.

If you have the use of a computer, you may have some basic drawing programs on it that will generate geometric shapes that you can cut out and use to make motifs. You can also find downloadable files on the Internet that can be printed out and used as templates for building motifs.

TRACING MOTIFS

Tracing paper is a great tool to use when developing motif ideas. If you aren't comfortable with drawing, purchase a pad of tracing paper to help you learn how to draw. Place tracing paper on top of a photograph or an illustration. With a pencil, transfer the important parts to the paper by tracing the shapes from the source material. Remove the tracing paper and then fine-tune the drawing to your liking by adding or removing parts of it that do not suit your desired end product. Some printing and painting techniques work best with basic shapes (foam stamping) and some can handle finer details (linoleum block print stamps). Here's how I build a motif from a photo.

1. Find a photograph to be your design inspiration. I used a picture of a zinnia from my garden (1). Place the tracing paper on top of the photograph. Using a felt tip pen or pencil, trace around the shapes in the photograph.

2. Remove the photograph. Examine the lines you just drew and decide which ones should be removed and which ones are important to the motif's design (2). Lay another piece of tracing paper on top of your first illustration. Trace all the important elements.

3. Look at your second illustration. Think about how it can be simplified to produce a motif that will be suitable to the technique you will be using (3). For instance, stamped fabric needs a simpler design motif, but linoleum block carving can handle finer details.

4. Continue tracing and eliminating elements until you have a motif that is simple enough for the technique (4).

FOLDING AND CUTTING MOTIFS

Sometimes I stumble upon a technique that has so many possibilities that I am surprised I hadn't done it sooner. When I was planning on stamping a design on a wall several years ago, I had to design a motif to use. Instinctively, I started drawing shapes that were a combination of organic and geometric designs—straight and curved lines. I realized that if I went back to the tried-and-true method of cutting a six-sided or eight-sided snowflake, I would get a precise repetitive motif on all sides with no measuring. For an evening I sat folding paper and cutting shape after shape after shape. I couldn't stop because each shape was prettier than the last.

Although I knew I was not the first person to discover this method for building a motif, I felt I was a genius. The possibilities were endless, and it was so easy! If you think you cannot draw, get out some paper and scissors and start folding and cutting. The cutting action is less scary than putting a pencil to paper for the drawing challeneged.

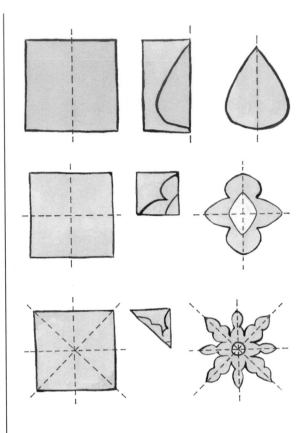

LOOKING FOR INSPIRATION

When you are just beginning to design patterns, it can be very overwhelming. A good way to learn about making patterns is to first observe. I am constantly looking at magazines, websites, and design books and visiting museums and historic homes. I can spend hours looking at photos—picking out the bits and pieces from a photo that make a room interesting or beautiful or perhaps neither.

Seek out and analyze fabrics or decorative papers that are covered with pattern. Each pattern is made up of a series of different shapes. Some fabrics are simple and orderly. Some patterns are very complex and full of all kinds of odd shapes.

I have a large collection of sourcebooks that I frequently turn to when designing my own patterns. A quick look at a pattern gives me a little crumb of information that I turn into my own design. I subscribe to many interior design magazines that feature beautiful photos of fabrics, tiles, flooring, and more that become fodder for my own designs. Most major museums, including the Victoria and Albert in London and the Metropolitan Museum of Art in New York City, have their collections available online. Browse their websites for ideas. Pinterest is full of millions of photos of patterns. As you can see, there is no lack of inspiration sources. Here is a list of some of my favorite sourcebooks and magazines:

Selvedge magazine

World of Interiors magazine

Elle Décor magazine (many countries)

Owen Jones's *Grammar of Ornament*

Auguste Racinet's *Historic Ornament L'Ornement Polychrome Series 1 and 2*

Susan Meller and Joost Elffers's *Textile Design*

DESIGNING WITH PATTERNS

When I first began learning to decorate, I was a bit fearful of mixing patterns together. I had seen it done in interior design magazines, but when it came to doing it myself, I wasn't sure I could pull it off. Then I did what I always do, I jumped in and gave it a try. And that is what you should do too. Here's an easy way to begin.

Begin with either a color or a patterned textile. Whichever one you choose, use it as a starting point that can guide the design of the rest of the room.

If you begin with a color, look for fabrics that you can use that will match the color, have the same color story, or have some of the color in it. Begin collecting fabrics and then decide on the color of the walls and the woodwork. Think about how the floors will be treated—covered with rugs, tiled, painted, or left as bare wood? Designing a room is an evolving process. A room will morph and change over the years as you add and subtract objects, but that is the fun of it.

If you begin with a textile, find a swatch of fabric that you really love love love—let's call it the "love fabric." Look for a bold print, a world textile, a patterned rug, or a colorful wallpaper.

Bold and complex patterns will present more possibilities when you choose coordinating patterns. The piece of fabric does not have to be large; it could be an exotic textile from a faraway land that will become a pillow.

NOTE: Most fabric retailers will give you small samples of fabrics that are helpful when designing a space. I find it helpful to purchase a half yard of a fabric that catches my eye and "live with it" in my space. That way I know if I really do love the fabric. A half yard is not a waste—it is enough for a pillow or two.

Identify the colors in your love fabric. Let the colors in the fabric help you to determine the wall color or treatment (wallpaper or borders).

Look for a few more prints with colors that are similar to your love fabric and use them for your couch, chairs, curtains, and pillows. Look for graphic choices such as a plaid or a check or a polka dot. It is good to pick patterns of different scale (bigness and smallness of a design). For instance, if you pick a huge plaid design, look for a smaller graphic pattern to mix in with the group. Find a solid fabric with a little bit of texture to add to the mix. It could be used to cover a couch

or chair. The texture in the design will add some more pattern, albeit it a subtler one. Don't worry about having the shades of colors in each fabric match exactly. It is more interesting if colors are a bit off. Less "matchy-matchy" will make a space look as if the room has evolved over time and be more interesting in the end.

Look for some trims that pick up the colors. Woven ribbons, pom-poms, braids, or fringe will add a bit of fun to any room. They can be added to solid-colored pillows, sewn on the borders of patterned pillows, or tacked to the edge of a curtain or the bottom of a chair.

Finally, look for a floor covering that will work with both the walls and the furniture. Designing a room is like a giant art project. Instead of paints and brushes, fabrics, furniture, rugs, and more create your palette.

When designing your space, also consider the function of the room. I live on a working sheep farm with dogs, cats, and farm animals. Choosing fabrics and colors for our home means that I have to find items that will stand up to constant wear. White doesn't work in our home, but maybe it will in yours. Patterned textiles are the perfect choice for our lifestyle because they hide dirt and withstand a rugged life. Jacquard woven fabrics (fabrics that have the design woven in as opposed to printed upon) are very sturdy. It is always a challenge to pick a fabric that will hold up for many years.

When designing your own space, start with a feeling. What do you want the room to feel like? How is the room going to be used? Is it a high-traffic hallway that is a conduit from one place to another? Is it going to be comfy and cozy? Is it going to be used just for good—for entertaining and show? Is it going to be used for eating and drinking and for throwing a party? Is it going to be used for sleeping? Is it a room for peace and perhaps meditation? Think about the people who will be living in the space and using the room. Ask them what they like and don't like. Think about what they do and how they live and work.

Each room in my house began in just this way. In my living room, I wanted to create a room that would stimulate conversation, be fun for entertaining, be cozy when knitting alone in front of the fire or intimate when reading a book or writing letters at the library table. To create the room, I began with a color—a pretty gold color I saw in Italy—and then looked for things that could be added to create the feeling I was looking for. The room is very long so I broke it up into different spaces—a sitting area in front of the fireplace, a library area on the west end, and a hallway area.

My space is a large room that is full of patterns that do not match each other. By choosing things that have common colors and mixing them all together, I created an interesting environment. Rooms like this don't happen overnight. It takes years of collecting and layering of patterns and objects to create such a space. That is the fun of decorating with patterns—adding new things when you find just the perfect fit.

USING COLOR IN YOUR PATTERNED HOME

All of the patterns featured in this book have a common theme—they are constructed using colors. Color defines pattern. It can be used boldly, like in my dining room, or it can be used quietly, as seen in the bathroom. To begin, we need to look at how colors work together.

My favorite way to look at all colors together is with an artist's color wheel. Once you are familiar with how it works, you will be able to use it as a guide for combining colors. A color wheel looks like a pie that is cut into twelve slices of color. The shades migrate around the wheel and look like a rainbow in the round. Red is next to red orange. Red orange is next to orange. Orange is next to yellow orange and so forth.

Different types of color combinations can be observed just by looking at the wheel. Using these combinations will produce different feelings and results.

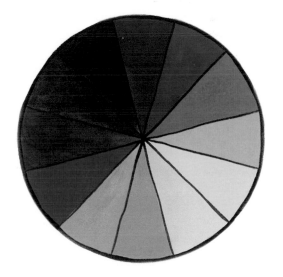

An easy way to learn about how colors work together is to isolate them one against the other. In the photos shown on this page, a small piece of yellow linen is placed on top of several different shades. When you look at the yellow, you will notice that it looks totally different in each photo. That change is the result of how your eyes are reacting to the color placement of the two colors. It is a fascinating exercise, and one you can learn from immediately and use often when designing patterns.

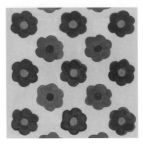

Colors that are next to each other on the color wheel are called analogous. This term means that they are similar to each other. Examples of analogous colors are red, red orange, orange yellow, and yellow. Patterns using analogous colors will create a calm and peaceful pattern. The pattern will not be earth-shaking but subtle. In our home, the Sunflower Bedroom uses the analogous colors of yellows and greens.

18

COMPLEMENTARY COLOR COMBINATION

Colors that are opposite each other on the color wheel are called complementary. This means they are not alike. Using complementary colors in patterns creates visual tension. The eye bounces from one color to the other and is excited. Complementary combinations are my very favorites—I find them happy and joyous. They are often found in nature. Pansy flowers (violet and yellow), coleus leaves (red and green), and the Southwest desert (blue sky with red rocks) are all examples of nature's use of complementary colors. In our home, the library uses complementary colors of red and green on the hand-painted walls.

TONAL COLOR COMBINATION

A tonal color combination is one that uses different tones or shades (lightness and darkness) of the same color in a pattern. An example of a tonal combination would be combining a pale blue with a dark navy blue. The difference in the tonal values will accentuate the pattern and the effect will be calmer and similar to an analogous color combination. Examples of tonal combinations in my living room are found in my use of the color green on the woodwork, the adjoining green walls, and striated chartreuse wall where it meets the bookcase.

If you want a space that is peaceful and tranquil, combine colors that are close to each other on the color wheel (analogous) or choose one color and use it in dark and light tones (tonal). These combinations will give a subtle look to the space. If you want a room that is joyful and stimulates creative conversation, choose complementary colors. The overall feeling will be bold and bright and energizing.

Working with color can be challenging at first. The more you play with and combine colors, the more comfortable you will become. Start by looking around you for color combinations that you like. Copy those combinations in your patterns.

Then go one step further and add different colors to the mix.

Working with colored markers and paint is another simple way to become more comfortable with combining colors. Purchase an inexpensive set of markers and some paper. Take an afternoon and just play with the colors. Draw stripes, polka dots, and other simple patterns in different color combinations. Vary the tones and combine similar colors. Begin by combining three or four colors and see what you can come up with. Experimentation is the first step—and an easy one—to move toward becoming bolder and more comfortable with working with colors and patterns.

FLORAL INSPIRATION
FOR PATTERN AND ROOM DESIGN

I make still lifes of things I own to help me design a pattern "colorway" (an industry term for a combination of colors; often a commercial pattern is available in several colorways), or design a room. Still lifes are similar to a mood board of photos, but they feature real-life color combinations. For a good creative still life exercise, try this:

Gather flowers from your garden or the farmers market. Bring them home and arrange them in a nice vase or jug. Look for a pretty backdrop, then set the vase in front of it. Find a patterned piece of fabric to add to the setting. Take a photo of the still life with your phone. Examine the photo and see how all the elements work together. Use the still life as an inspiration for your next room design or pattern.

TECHNIQUES AND TOOLS

To create my patterned home, I learned many different techniques that I employed in its decoration. When I was a child, my mother and grandmother taught me embroidery, sewing, crochet, and knitting. When my husband and I purchased our first home, I taught myself how to paint and colorwash walls and furniture. I learned how to mix fabrics and patterns together to create a warm and inviting home by trial and error. Later on, I taught myself how to make stamps to print fabric and walls. Through my career, I was lucky to learn computer skills including Adobe Illustrator and Photoshop. I learned to make pottery at an adult education course. Now, when I am interested in learning a new skill, I turn first to YouTube, Creativebug, Craftsy, and Skillshare. There are so many techniques out there to learn and experiment with—it just takes motivation plus the urge to get over your fears and just do it.

Over the years, I have amassed a collection of supplies and tools that I use over and over. Some of the supplies will last a lifetime, and some will need to be replenished. Lots of tools can be picked up for relatively little money if you keep your eyes open and shop at yard sales, thrift stores, estate sales, and auctions. Soon you will be adding jigsaws and paintbrushes to your wish list.

PAINTING

Painting is one of the easiest and most economical ways to add color and pattern to a home. I've painted walls, furniture, floors, bathtubs, and more. Many different techniques use paint to make patterns—colorwashing, dragging, masking, combing, freehand painting and stamping, and creating pattern templates. Some are very easy to do, and some require more skill. The common theme running throughout all the techniques is that each uses paint to create a patterned surface.

The first time you try to paint a pattern on a wall or a piece of furniture, it will be a bit scary. Each time you add a pattern with a paint technique, your confidence will increase and it will become easier and easier. By the fourth or fifth time, you won't even think about the mistakes you might make. So if you're new to painting, just get on with it and don't think too much about it. (In our bathroom, I added the design to the bathtub

Rust Reformer and spray paint

Artist's acrylic paint

in less than an hour.) The great thing about adding painted pattern to your home is that you can easily cover up a project that perhaps didn't work out. Experience is the best teacher—so just begin!

PAINT

I keep many kinds of paint in my studio and all have a different use. Some types can be used for multiple crafts. These are the different types of paint I use frequently.

LATEX PAINTS. I used latex paint for many of the projects in this book. The soap-and-water cleanup is easy. I purchase the small tester size 8-ounce jars because they are relatively inexpensive and I can have many colors on hand. I stack the jars in my studio bookcase, marking each jar on the outside with a stripe of paint so that I can easily grab a color.

Latex paint comes in several finishes: matte, eggshell, satin, semi-gloss, high-gloss, and floor/

patio paint. Generally, the more shine a finish has, the more durable it will be. I prefer semi-gloss for woodwork and furniture and satin for walls. For floors, I always use floor paint because it is much more durable than any other finish.

OIL-BASED PAINT. I used oil-based paint on most of the woodwork our home. It is extremely durable and can be washed easily. Oil-based paint takes a complete day to dry, so you have to plan your projects accordingly. It is quite smelly, and it takes many days for the smell to go away. Oil-based paint is getting more difficult to purchase because of environmental regulations, but if you want the most durable paint, choose oil-based paint. Rustoleum is an oil-based paint that is available in small containers and in many colors. It works well for signs and outdoor furniture. Many of the surfaces in our home that I painted with oil-based paint are still holding up after almost twenty years without repainting.

Latex paint

ARTIST'S ACRYLICS. I used artist's acrylics for many of the projects in this book. Many different brands are available in both student and professional grades. Student-grade paints have less pigment and are less expensive; professional-grade paints are highly pigmented but cost more. I prefer Golden and Liquitex brands.

Artist's acrylic paints can be intermixed with latex paints from the hardware store. In my murals and wall treatments, I mix the two to develop the colors I need. I store the mixed colors in deli and sour cream containers with tight-fitting lids so they will not dry out.

Craft stores sell acrylic paints in 2-ounce bottles with snap-on lids that make pouring easy. These acrylics are available in different finishes and come in many colors, which is handy for those who fear mixing their own colors. They can be mixed with latex and artist's acrylic paints. This is a more expensive way to purchase paint, but the containers are smaller and do not take up as much space as paint from the hardware store. The 2-ounce size often costs the same as an 8-ounce tester jar. They are very convenient and will take up less storage space.

SPRAY PAINT. Recently the DIY market has seen an explosion in the number of colors and finishes available in spray paint. Spray paint can now be used on metal, wood, plastic, vinyl, and more. Use spray paint outside or in a ventilated garage to avoid inhaling fumes. If you're painting outside, try to pick a day without wind. When spray painting, use short blasts of paint so that the piece is painted with several thin layers; the paint will pool if the layers are too thick. Spray paint is oil based and very durable. It is perfect for outdoor furniture and for pieces with nooks and crannies, such as baskets or wicker furniture, that might take too long to paint with a brush.

RUST REFORMER. Although not a paint, Rust Reformer is a spray product that bonds rusty metal, making it into a matte black, non-rusting surface. Originally developed for the automobile repair market, Rust Reformer lets you skip sanding away rust. After the product dries, the surface can be painted with spray paint or brushed on latex or oil-based paints. I used it in many of the metal projects in this book, and they look like new once painted.

PAINT TIPS

Paint will eventually dry out and usually does not age well. Keep that in mind when you make a purchase so that you don't toss lots of money and nasty chemical-based products away. It is easy to be tempted to buy more paint than you need when it is on sale, but what will you do with it when there is a huge amount left over?

- After using paint, make sure to put the lid back on very tightly so it won't dry out. To discard paint, line a box with a plastic bag and pour the paint in. After a few days, it will be a solid mass and can be thrown in the trash. Make sure to keep your pets away from drying paint so they don't spread it all over your house or garage.
- Look for organizations that might need some paint and donate your leftovers.

- The general rule for layering different types of paint is that you can paint latex over oil primer or paint but you should not paint oil over latex primer or paint.
- When washing up latex paint, try to do it outside. Don't dump the rinse water down the sink as the latex can build up in your water pipes.
- To clean up oil-based paint, use paint thinner.
- You can create glazes for translucent color-wash effects with both oil-based and latex paints. Thin oil-based paint with paint thinner and thin latex paint with water.

PAINTBRUSHES

PAINTBRUSHES FOR INTERIORS. For painting walls and furniture, I purchase paintbrushes recommended by the manufacturer of the type of paint I am using. I use both synthetic and natural bristle brushes. I always have a supply of the inexpensive natural bristle chip brushes on hand. Although most people throw them away, I use them over and over. They are especially useful for putting on a thin layer of paint when you are doing decorative painting and you want the different layers to show through. When brand new, brushes will shed their bristles. Check your painted surface and remove any stray bristles before they dry into the paint.

I love foam brushes, and I have them in a variety of sizes—from a very small cosmetic size to 2 inches wide. If you wash them out every time, they will last for years.

DECORATIVE PAINTING BRUSHES. Many brushes specially designed for decorative painting can be quite expensive. I usually make do with normal paintbrushes for larger jobs. I do find the small foam circular dauber brushes to be really useful for fabric painting and for decorative painting on furniture. Stippling brushes are also good for decorative painting.

ARTIST'S BRUSHES. You can spend huge amounts of money on artist's brushes, but I don't. Over the years, I have become very fond of the inexpensive craft brushes made of taklon fibers. Purchase a selection of different sizes to have on hand, including round brushes, flat brushes, and liner brushes. I use them for painting furniture, ceramics, and fabrics. Frequently, you can find mixed brush packs for sale at craft stores with a selection of sizes and types of brushes, which gives you a great opportunity to experiment with different sizes, shapes, and styles of brushes. Clean your brushes well and they will last a long time.

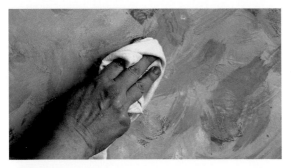

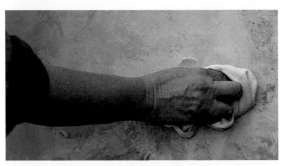

BASIC TECHNIQUE: COLORWASHING

Colorwashing is an easy decorative painting technique that I used throughout our home. I like this technique because it gives a moody quality to the finished wall, stairway, or furniture. The technique is similar to those used in fine art painting. By layering colors on top of each other with varying degrees of coverage, a soft, textured-looking surface results. This technique is good for high-traffic areas as it hides dirt and scuffs better than solid-colored walls. Like all art projects, you'll need a certain degree of faith to continue as the colors look sloppy as they are being applied. The final wash of color will unify the look and hold it all together visually. The nice thing about colorwashing is it can be refreshed with additional layers of paint as it wears. Make sure to save your paint and label it so you will remember what colors you used.

SUPPLIES

Latex paint in at least three colors (see note)

Roller

1-inch brush

Plastic paint containers

Rags

Polyurethane, optional

NOTE: For the base coat behind, I used a light blue. The wall was then colorwashed in several different colors. The top finish coat was turquoise. When you look at the wall, it looks mostly turquoise with only bits of the other colors showing through where the top layer is more transparent. When choosing colors, remember that the base and middle colors will not show too much on the finished wall. They give interest and depth to the finished color. You really can choose any color you like, although I suggest staying with a similar tone (darkness or lightness). If you were to paint a wall a pastel color, add bits of black as the second layer, and then do a pastel color as the top layer, the black would look splodgy and unattractive. It is impossible to make a mistake with this technique as you can always add extra layers of colors if you don't like the initial result. It is helpful to decide upon the colors you want to use and then practice on a piece of cardboard to see if you are going to like the end result.

1. Apply the base coat with a brush or roller. I used light blue. Let the paint dry.

2. Pour a small amount of the middle layer color(s) into a large paint container. I used blue, amber, light green, and gray. Thin it with water until it is the consistency of heavy cream. With a rag, and using a sweeping motion, wash the wall with the first wash color. To give more texture, make sure to leave some areas uncovered or lightly colored. At this point, you can continue to add extra layers of different colors to give a more complex look to the finished wall. Let the paint dry.

3. Choose a color for the top layer. I used turquoise. Dilute the color with water to the consistency of heavy cream. Soak a rag with the final color. Using large sweeping motions, wash the walls with the paint. Near the trim, use a smaller rag or a brush and take care to be neat. Let the paint dry. Do a second coat of paint if you want a more opaque look.

4. For high-traffic areas such as floors, cover the surface with polyurethane to seal it.

PRINTING AND STAMPING

Printing is the most common technique for adding surface design to an object. Although most printed things in your home are printed by machine, it is very easy to print items yourself by hand. I hand print on fabrics in the projects in this book, but you can also print on paper, walls, and floors. Printing can be as simple as stamping with a single motif, or you can combine many motifs to make a more complex design.

TEXTILE PAINTS

FABRIC PAINTS FOR FABRIC. Several brands of paints are available just for textiles. I prefer those made by Jacquard Products over the fabric paint brands that are available at craft stores. Jacquard paints have a much softer hand. "Hand" is a term for the feel of the fabric. Craft store fabric paints yield a stiffer, less natural feeling and less drapey fabric. Fabric paints are available in opaque, translucent, and metallic finishes, and I mostly use the translucent type called Jacquard Textile Color. All fabric paints clean up easily with water. The colors are quite bright. If you want a lighter shade, thin the paint with Jacquard's Colorless Extender so that the body and texture of the paint and its translucency are not altered. If you thin the paints with water, they will bleed and run. Fabric paints need to be heat-set when dry, but a product called Versatex Fabric Fixer eliminates the need for heat-setting.

LATEX PAINT FOR FABRICS. Ordinary latex house paint can be used to paint and print fabric too. I used the matte finish for many of the projects in

Fabric paint

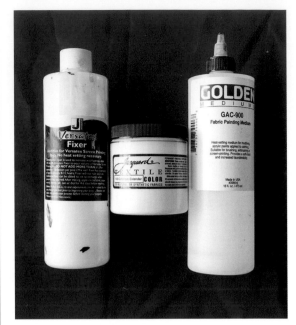

Color fixer, extender, and medium

Printing inks for fabric

this book. Printing with latex will give an opaque finish (the fabric color below the paint will not show through the layer of paint). To use latex for fabric printing, mix it with fabric medium to make the paint softer and more pliable. Follow the manufacturer's directions for mixing. If you don't want to heat-set your project, add Versatex Fixer to make the color permanent. All printed and painted fabrics should cure for five days before washing.

BLOCK PRINTING INKS AND SCREEN PRINTING INKS FOR FABRIC. Block printing inks are made by several manufacturers. I use Speedball Fabric and Paper Block Printing Ink, which is oil based but washable with soap and water. This paint has the consistency of toothpaste and should be spread with a brayer (a roller with a firm rubber surface) on an inking surface such as a palette or piece of Plexiglas. The resulting print is crisp and defined. Once printed onto fabric, the ink needs several days to dry and cure before you use and wash the item. No heat-setting is required. Block printing inks can also be used on paper.

Several brands of screen printing inks can be used for block printing. I use Versatex Screen Printing Ink, which is recommended for block printing. This ink is thicker than fabric paints, has an opaque finish, and is basically the same formula as fabric paint. It produces a print that is a bit soft and fuzzy. The ink needs to be heat-set when dry. Screen printing ink can be used for foam stamping as well. Use a foam roller to roll the paint onto a stamp to create some friction.

STAMPING AND PRINTING SUPPLIES

I use two different types of stamp materials for printing. For linoleum block printing, I prefer the Speedy-Carve pink blocks from Speedball. They carve very easily and smoothly. The blocks are a bit thin and will last longer if you mount them on acrylic mounts or builder's insulation foam. Speedball also makes the Speedy-Cut brand that is a little thicker and longer lasting but also more expensive. Use it for stamps you think you will be using for years.

I use craft foam with an adhesive backing (available at craft stores) to make simpler stamps for printing on fabric and more. Make sure you purchase the craft foam with adhesive. These stamps will be durable through many prints—I printed 9 yards of fabric with one foam stamp (see the Paisley Hand-Printed Upholstered Chair project on page 83).

Linoleum block stamps, carving tools, and brayer

Craft foam stamps

After each printing session, wash the blocks with soap and water. Latex paint will dry out the foam. If you forget the cleanup, don't worry. Making the craft foam printing stamps is very easy and economical, so you can always remake a design.

STAMPING TIPS

1. Have some water available to rinse foam brushes and a sponge to wash stamps when you change colors.

2. Always do a trial stamp or two on a scrap of fabric before beginning on your project. You want to make sure that the stamp is completely covered with paint to guarantee good paint coverage when you start stamping.

3. To line up stamps to keep the pattern evenly spaced on foam stamps, draw vertical and horizontal lines through the exact center of each stamp with a permanent marker. Continue the lines up the sides of the foam. Then draw the horizontal and vertical lines across the back of the foam stamp. These visual crosshairs will help you center the motifs.

4. Use guides for spacing your motifs. Cut and place small bits of cardboard between the stamps to determine spacing. I often use yardsticks or long pieces of wood.

5. Water soluble and auto-fade fabric markers (sold at quilting stores) are also useful for drawing guidelines directly on the fabric. Draw a line using a ruler as a guide and print along the guide.

6. An apron or smock will keep your clothes clean.

7. A hair dryer is handy to quickly dry paint on walls and paper. It is best to let paint on fabric dry naturally.

8. Use rags to wipe off mistakes on walls, floors, and furniture. It is impossible to remove printing mistakes from fabric.

9. Make sure you clean your stamps. Latex paint will dry out the foam, and the stamps will become stiff and unusable.

10. To avoid heat-setting of printed designs, add Versatex Fixer to your fabric paint. It will remain active in wet paint for 4 to 6 hours. Refresh your paint with more fixer if you are printing over several hours.

BLOCK PRINTING TIPS

1. Block printing is a good choice for fabric printing when a crisp and more detailed design is desired. It takes a few more tools than printing with craft foam but is worth the extra work.

2. Make sure you clean your block with soap and water. If you leave ink on it, the block will dry out and crack.

3. Blocks can be mounted on acrylic mounts, wood, or builder's insulation foam. Blocks are a little easier to handle when mounted. They will also last longer because they will be sturdier.

4. Draw guidelines on the back of the block to help you line up the printing impressions. Using a permanent marker, draw a horizontal and vertical line in the exact center of the back

of the block. These visual crosshairs will help you center the motifs.

5. Use guides for spacing your motifs. Cut and place small bits of cardboard between the prints to determine spacing. I often use yardsticks or long pieces of wood for printing in rows.

6. Water soluble and auto-fade markers (sold at quilting stores) are also useful for drawing guidelines on fabric. Draw a line using a ruler as a guide and print along the guide.

BASIC TECHNIQUE: MAKING STAMPS

Fabric printing (or stamping) with craft foam is one of my favorite ways to decorate. It is very inexpensive to do, and the supplies are easily available. To think that I can make sophisticated-looking fabric with craft foam mounted on builder's foam insulation is pretty amazing. The foam is easy to cut with scissors, and the detail you can get is endless depending on your patience. Purchase the craft foam with the adhesive backing because it is much easier to mount than messing with glue and waiting for it to dry.

If you choose to print a design that has a second and third layer of color, use an acrylic mounting block so that you can see exactly where you are stamping. They are available online through stamping suppliers or can be cut at specialty glass stores from Plexiglas.

SUPPLIES

Craft foam with adhesive backing

Motif template (see "Templates" on page 165 or make your own)

Scissors

Tape

1-inch foam insulation board available at building supply stores in 4 × 8-foot sheets

Acrylic see-through stamp mounts (optional)

Utility knife

1. To make the stamp, enlarge the template as given or draw your own motif (see "Making Patterns" on page 10). Cut out the paper template. Using tape, attach it to a piece of craft foam with adhesive backing. Cut the motif out of the craft foam.

2. Remove the paper from the adhesive backing on the foam. Push firmly to stick the foam motif to the foam insulation or acrylic mount.

3. When exact pattern registration is not necessary, use builder's foam insulation for your mount. To trim the insulation board close to the stamping motif, use a sharp utility knife and make a shallow cut around the motif. Snap the foam by resting it on the edge of a table and it will break along the cut.

4. When you need to see where you are stamping, as for a complex floral design, mount your foam stamp on an acrylic see-through mount. You can have these mounts made at glass supply stores or purchase them online. In a pinch, a clear CD case will work too.

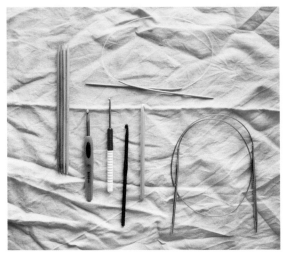

Needles for knitting and crochet

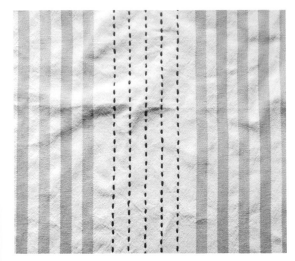

Fabric to embroider

STITCHING

Making things with thread, needle, and fabric has been a lifelong passion of mine. Learning basic sewing, embroidery, knitting, and crochet is a way to add warmth and individuality to your home. These domestic arts are experiencing a huge revival in interest and are perfect crafts to fit into your daily life. Most of the stitching arts can be quickly learned and are a perfect way to add patterned decoration to your home. The satisfaction you will feel when displaying and using your hand-stitched items is irreplaceable.

FABRIC
I have been sewing clothing and things for my home since I was nine years old. I prefer natural fiber fabrics to synthetic fabrics and especially love hand sewing and embroidering on cotton, linen, and wool. As a frequenter of tag sales and flea markets, I am always on the lookout for vintage fabrics in the form of tablecloths, curtains, and blankets. The fabric is always of a higher quality than is

available today. If a piece is stained, the section can be worked around, dyed, or embroidered.

VINTAGE AND WORLD EMBROIDERED AND HANDMADE TEXTILES
I have always been surrounded by fabrics that have been made by hand. My early fascination with handmade textiles began with the crocheted, tatted, embroidered, and quilted pieces made by my grandmother and great-grandmother. When I went to college, I caught the world textile bug and began collecting embroidered fabrics from faraway lands. I was enamored with the small, intricate, hand-done stitches; the interesting motifs; and the beautiful color combinations. I am always scouting for handmade textiles at yard sales, flea markets, and thrift stores—whether made in this country or from other cultures. If a piece is damaged or a remnant of a larger piece, it can be used for a pillow or wall hanging. Our home is filled with many pillows made from world textiles I have collected over the years.

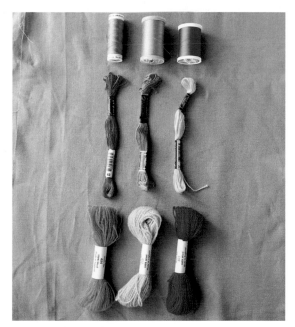
Sewing and embroidery threads

Yarn for knitting and crochet

THREADS AND NEEDLES

For embroidery, I use both mercerized cotton and crewel and tapestry wool embroidery threads. For beginning stitchers, wool embroidery threads are more forgiving. I prefer chenille needles for embroidery because the eye is large and easy to thread.

YARN AND TOOLS FOR KNITTING AND CROCHET

For knitting and crochet, I prefer 100 percent wool yarn or those that are blends of wool, mohair, and alpaca fibers. These fibers take dyes beautifully and have great depth of color. Needles and hooks are available in metal, wood, and plastic, and I like to use all three materials.

BASIC TECHNIQUE: MAKING NAPKINS

Napkins come in different sizes: 13-inch square for cocktails, 18-inch square for luncheon, and 22-inch square for dinner. Look for vintage fabrics at yard sales and flea markets, as they make great napkins. They have a nice texture because they have already been used. If they are stained, you can dye them or print over the stain to hide it. Purchase ready-made napkins if you don't want to make them yourself.

HOW TO MAKE FRINGED NAPKINS

1. Using scissors and a ruler, cut 18 × 18-inch squares from the fabric. One-half yard of 54-inch fabric will yield 3 napkins. Vary the size of the napkins depending on the width of the fabric.

2. Using sewing thread that matches the fabric and a sewing machine, sew a straight stitch ½ inch in from the edge all the way around the napkin.

3. Using a straight pin, unweave the horizontal threads along each of the 4 sides of the napkin. Pull the threads one by one until you reach the stitching. If the thread is caught in the stitching in the middle of the napkin, trim it off next to the stitching. Continue unweaving and pulling threads around all 4 sides.

HOW TO MAKE HEMMED NAPKINS

1. Cut 14-inch, 19-inch, or 23-inch squares out of your chosen fabric. Use a rotary cutter and quilting ruler to make a straight edge if desired.

2. Turn the edge under ⅛ inch all the way around and press with a steam iron. Turn each edge under ⅜ inch and press again. Using a sewing machine, sew along the inside folded edges, close to the fold.

BASIC TECHNIQUE:
MAKING AN EASY THROW PILLOW

Throw pillows are one of the easiest ways to introduce pattern and color into a space. To gain confidence with mixing different types of patterns together, make some pillow covers in different designs for your couch. They can be easily switched out by season or changed once you tire of the fabric designs. This method makes a pillow cover with an envelope back that can easily be removed for quick laundering. No zipper required.

I prefer down and feather-blend pillows because they squish better and are more comfortable to sit against. They also can be puffed up quickly and will last forever. When mine need a refresher, I wash them in the washing machine and dry them in the dryer. I've been lucky to find some at yard sales lurking under some old and tattered covers. Polyester fiberfill pillows will flatten and become lumpy quickly.

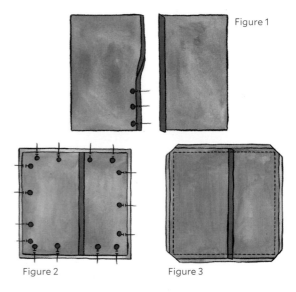

Figure 1

Figure 2

Figure 3

1. Pillows come in the following square sizes: 12 inches, 14 inches, 16 inches, 18 inches, and 20 inches. Rectangular sizes are 12 × 16-inch, 16 × 20-inch, and 20 × 24-inch. I find that a 14- to 18-inch pillow is a good size for a couch. Cut the fabric for the front of the pillow 1 inch larger than the pillow insert size to allow for seam allowances.

2. Cut the backing fabric 3 inches wider than the pillow front and the same height. Fold the piece in half widthwise and cut along the fold.

3. Lay the 2 pillow back pieces side by side, right side down. (See Figure 1.) Fold the center edges under ⅛ inch to the wrong side and press. Fold under again ⅜ inch and press. Hand or machine stitch a hem in place along the inside fold.

4. Lay the front piece right side up on a table. Place 1 backing piece with its right side facing the decorated piece; make sure the hemmed edge is in the center of the pillow and line up the outside edges. (See Figure 2.) Pin it in place. Lay the other backing piece on top with the hemmed edge in the center of the pillow, lining up the outside edges. Pin it in place. The pieces will overlap in the middle.

5. Sew around all 4 sides of the pillow, making a ½-inch seam all the way around. (See Figure 3.) For neat corners, clip all 4 corners diagonally to remove excess fabric. Turn the pillow right side out. Use a knitting needle or capped pen to push out the corners from inside the pillow. Press to flatten the seams. Insert the pillow form.

DIGITAL PRINTING

Because this is a book on pattern, I would be remiss if I did not mention the digital printing possibilities that are now available. Spoonflower is the most popular digital printer for DIY-ers. It offers many different fabric types—including linen/cotton canvas that is perfect for interiors. Spoonflower also prints on wallpaper and wrapping paper.

There are many books on designing fabrics for digital printing and online classes too. Although it is helpful if you have computer skills, including Adobe Illustrator and Photoshop, they are not necessary. You can upload a simple drawing to the Spoonflower website, and it will allow you to put it into several different repeat patterns—straight, drop, brick, single, and mirror. Any of the many online video tutorials will help get you started.

OTHER SUPPLIES

CUTTING AND CARVING TOOLS

I have a supply of different kinds of scissors—kids' craft scissors, sharp and pointy metal scissors, kitchen scissors, and scissors that I only use for fabrics. I try to avoid using fabric scissors with non-fiber materials as they are easily dulled and ruined.

For cutting foam, I use craft scissors, sharp scissors, and X-Acto knives. For cutting linoleum blocks, I use linoleum carving tools. When you are just beginning, purchase a set of assorted carving heads that are housed in a hollow handle.

Scissors for cutting fabric, paper, and foam

TEMPLATES AND RULERS

Many of the projects in this book require templates or rulers to transfer designs. You may not want to follow my designs exactly, and I urge you to put your own spin on my projects.

You have many things in your own home that you can use as templates. If you need a circle, look for a jar or lid of the size you need. If you need a rectangle, trace around a book or a box. Scour your house for other shape ideas for building patterns. What about a deck of cards or a ruler? You probably have many things you can use somewhere in your very own home.

A quilting ruler is clear and has a grid marked on it. I find all kinds of uses for mine and have them in several sizes.

OPTIONAL TOOLS THAT ARE USEFUL

I turn to many tools again and again when decorating my home: electric drill, builder's level, paint trays, orbital sander, hacksaw, jigsaw, hammer, nails, screwdriver, and rotary tool from Dremel. It is also handy to have some drop cloths and plastic sheeting to protect your area when painting. Look for gently used tools at estate sales or online.

CERAMIC GLAZES

I use underglazes for painting my ceramic designs. Depending on the colors available, I use Amaco, Duncan, and Mayco brands. For the final coat of gloss glaze, I use Amaco lead-free, food-safe, clear glaze. Most pottery studios open to the public will have their own supplies of underglaze and glaze that you can use.

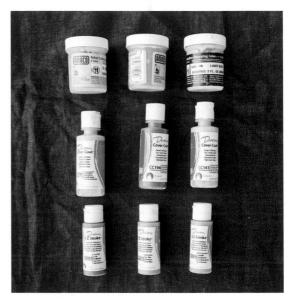

Ceramic underglazes

PART ONE

INDOOR SPACES

CHAPTER ONE

KITCHEN
AND
DINING ROOM

A KITCHEN IS A PLACE TO SHARE LOVE AND NOURISHMENT WITH FAMILY AND FRIENDS. IT SHOULD BE WELCOMING, SMELL DELICIOUS, AND BE FILLED WITH THINGS YOU LOVE. OUR FARMHOUSE KITCHEN WALLS ARE WOOD PANELING COVERED IN LIGHT GRAY PAINT, THE COLOR OF MORNING FOG. THEY ARE A subtle backdrop to the pieces of inherited furniture and colorful patterns that decorate the informal, hard-working space. On the walls, in the open shelves, and on the tabletop, I display and use antique and contemporary ceramics that I have acquired over the years on trips to flea markets and other countries. Some I have made myself. Small bits of pattern decorate each piece. When gathered together, the diverse patterns and shapes combine to give a feeling of a creative jumble.

The utilitarian things of kitchen life—dishes, glassware, pots, and pans, along with the large work table and wooden tabletop—make the kitchen extremely serviceable. An overstuffed wing chair covered in a cheerful linen fabric digitally printed from my own design is a favorite spot to sit and read. At the far end of the kitchen, a daybed is surrounded by two bookcases overflowing with cooking and farming books. A collection of my handmade pillows edge the cozy sitting and napping space. I rotate Indian block-printed cotton bedcovers through the year. These no-sew, colorful, patterned textiles change the feeling of the space as the seasons change. On the floors, I have Persian wool rugs that add warmth and texture to the space. The mishmash of patterns in the kitchen creates a lively, bright, and welcoming room where my family and I spend many hours.

The dining room's decoration has a completely different vibe. It is dark but colorful. The walls employ my favorite decorating scheme—pattern on pattern. An overblown hand-painted floral pattern is juxtaposed against a tartan plaid design that I painted. The decorative scheme was inspired by the Jacobean-style, carved, sturdy furniture inherited from my Great Aunt Jennie. The hand-painted flowers, leaves, birds, bugs, and guinea hens climb and nest over vines scattered across three walls. They are an ode to the crewel embroidery I love—popular in the Jacobean era (the 1600s) and the 1970s. The dark colors of the walls and furniture create a stimulating backdrop to the food, drink, and conversations we share with extended family and friends. An old-fashioned, non-electrified brass chandelier and candlesticks illuminate the room with warm, flattering light. Embroidered and patterned textiles from around the globe add an exotic flair and induce the urge to solve the problems of the world over candlelight, a bottle of wine, and a good meal.

Using pattern and color to different degrees in the kitchen and dining room gives an entirely different effect and feeling to each space. It is easy to add bits of handmade pattern as you live in your home to create a space that you will love more and more each year.

KANTHA-INSPIRED DISHTOWELS

> **PATTERN STYLE:** Geometric
> **PATTERN REPEAT:** Straight
> **TECHNIQUE:** Embroidery

Hand-embroidered dishtowels are a luxury that can turn a mundane task into a special event. These Kantha-Inspired Dishtowels are named after a traditional quilting technique done for hundreds of years by rural women in India. Using a simple running stitch, they sew layers of old saris together to create quilts and pillows. For this project, you will need striped dishtowels with a blank center panel that you will embroider. Fabric yardage for dishtowels like this can be found in quilting supply stores. Look for vintage towels at flea markets and yard sales. The running stitch can also be added to any striped dishtowel, decorating the different stripes with many colors. This project is very relaxing to do and makes lovely housewarming or shower gifts.

SUPPLIES

Cotton or linen dishtow-els with striped borders

Pearl cotton embroidery floss in size 5 (27 yards)

Chenille needle in size 20

Embroidery scissors

Auto-fade fabric marker

Quilting ruler with grid lines

Figure 1

1. Prewash the dishtowel and dry it in the dryer. Remove it before it is completely dry so the wrinkles do not set. Iron the fabric.

2. Using the quilting ruler, determine the vertical center point of the dishtowel. Lay the ruler along the point and, using the auto-fade fabric marker, draw a vertical line to act as a stitching guide.

3. Using the quilting ruler, draw a second line ½ to ¾ inch away from the centerline. Continue drawing vertical lines the same distance away from each other on each side of the centerline. My dishtowels had room for 5 vertical lines.

4. Measure the length of the dishtowel and cut 2 strands of embroidery thread 8 inches longer than this measurement.

5. Thread the needle with the 2 strands and place a knot approximately 1 inch from the end. Beginning at one end, work a running stitch on 1 vertical line. (See Figure 1.) The stitches should be approximately ¼ inch long. Cover the entire line of stitching. At the end of the line, pull the needle to the back of the towel, ¹⁄₁₆ inch from the edge. Make a knot in the last stitch on the top side of the towel to finish and secure the thread. Make a knot about 1 inch from the last stitch and cut the thread close to the knot.

6. Continue until all the lines have been stitched.

GEOMETRIC STRIPED TABLECLOTH

PATTERN STYLE: Geometric
PATTERN REPEAT: Straight
TECHNIQUE: Stamping

I love antiques and vintage pieces, but I also like contemporary design. A lot of modern textiles feature simple geometric shapes as their motifs. I thought it would be fun to mix a modern pattern aesthetic into our old-fashioned kitchen. This tablecloth features stripes of eleven different motifs made of little squares, rectangles, circles, octagons, ogees, and more. I used craft foam to make the printing stamps and printed the fabric with latex paint mixed with fabric medium. Shades of blue, turquoise, and dark brown mix nicely with all the antique jugs and pottery that are on display on the kitchen shelves. To make the project simpler, choose only three or four motifs to print.

SUPPLIES

FOR THE STAMPS

Templates A–K
(see pages 166–70)

Craft foam with adhesive backing

1-inch-thick foam building insulation

Scissors

Tape

Utility knife

FOR THE TABLECLOTH

100% cotton canvas
(see note)

Steam iron

Sewing machine

Sewing thread to match canvas

Drop cloth

Latex paints in several colors (see note)

Golden GAC 900 Fabric Painting Medium

Versatex Fixer, optional (see note)

½-inch and 1-inch foam brushes

Deli containers for holding paint

Large table for printing

Auto-fade fabric marker

Yardstick

Fabric and craft scissors

NOTE: For this project, I used latex house paint mixed with fabric medium rather than fabric paint to print the motifs. Latex paint is opaque and sits nicely on top of the stiff, durable, cotton canvas fabric. I used 5 colors: periwinkle, royal, turquoise, teal, and dark brown. The fabric medium requires you to heat-set the paint; if you'd like to avoid this step, add Versatex Fixer to the paint following the manufacturer's directions. My tablecloth is made from 3⅔ yards of 72-inch wide fabric (Dharma Trading's PFD [prepped for dyeing]) to make a tablecloth that measured 68 × 120 inches after washing and hemming.

1. Prewash the fabric and dry it in the dryer. Remove it before it is completely dry so the wrinkles do not set. Iron the fabric.

2. Hem the edges. Turn the fabric under ¼ inch and press. Then turn it under another ½ inch and press again. Sew with matching thread.

3. Prepare the stamps. Make stamps using Templates A to K for the little squares, hexagon, ogee, open circle, medium and small diamonds, split circle, quarter circle, large and small triangle, and stripes (see "Basic Technique: Making Stamps" on page 33).

4. Cover your work surface with a drop cloth.

5. Mix the latex paint with the fabric medium, following the manufacturer's directions. You will not need a lot of paint for each color. If you run out, you can always mix more. I begin by mixing 1 tablespoon of paint with 1 tablespoon of fabric medium. Add the Versatex Fixer (optional).

6. Using a graph ruler and auto-fade fabric marker, draw a horizontal line 3 inches in from and parallel to one short end of the tablecloth. This line will act as a guide for the prints. After each stripe is completed, draw another horizontal line 3 inches from the completed stripe to make the next line.

7. Beginning at one edge of the cloth, line up the edge of the motifs along the guideline. The end of the row may end up being a partial motif, depending on the size of each stamp.

8. Use the foam brush to apply paint to your stamps. Try a few sample stamps on some scrap fabric to get the feeling of the pressure needed. Press the stamp firmly onto the fabric, tapping on the back to transfer the paint to the fabric. I printed my stripes and stamps in this order:

- STRIPES—Print 2 rows of the motif, alternating the direction of the stripes and spaced ½ inch apart.

- LARGE TRIANGLES—Print 1 row with the narrow point facing up, spacing the motifs ½ inch apart. Print the second row of triangles ½ inch from the first with the point facing opposite the first row and filling in the space created in the first row.

- HEXAGONS AND SMALL DIAMONDS— Print 1 row of hexagons with a horizontal edge along the guideline, spacing the motifs ½ inch apart. Print a second row directly above the first, ½ inch apart. Print a small diamond centered in the open space between the hexagons.

- SPLIT CIRCLES—Print 1 row of split circles, spacing them ½ inch apart.

- LITTLE SQUARES—Print 1 row of little squares, spacing them ½ inch apart. Repeat with a second row directly above the first.

- QUARTER CIRCLES—Print 1 row of quarter circles, spaced ½ inch apart, with the round edge placed along the guideline and the point facing up. Print a second row of quarter circles opposite the first, filling in the open space.

- **LARGE DIAMONDS**—Print 1 row of diamonds lengthwise across the tablecloth, with the wider point placed along the guideline. The tips of the diamonds should just touch. Print a second row directly above the first with the tips touching.

- **HEXAGONS**—Print 1 hexagon with an edge along the guideline. Print a second hexagon just above it by ¼ inch. Next, print a hexagon ¼ inch away from the first two, placing a point in the space created by the first 2 hexagons. Continue across the row, repeating the placement.

- **SMALL DIAMONDS**—Print 1 row of small diamonds, ½ inch apart, with a point along the guideline. Print a second row of diamonds with the motif placed in the open space created by the first row.

- **OPEN CIRCLES**—Print 1 row of open circles, spacing them ½ inch apart.

- **OGEES**—Print 1 row of ogees, placing the rounded edge along the guideline with the points almost touching.

- **SMALL TRIANGLES**—Print 1 row of small triangles with a short edge along the guideline and the tips just touching. Repeat with 2 more rows of small triangles directly above the first.

9. Once the first stripe is finished, measure 3 inches away and draw a straight line using the ruler and the auto-fade fabric marker. Begin the second stripe with a different shape stamp and different color of paint following the order above.

10. Continue printing the entire cloth in this manner, changing motifs and colors as the fabric progresses. As the fabric is printed, it will be necessary to roll it up once it is dry so the unprinted section can remain on the table.

11. If you did not use the Versatex Fixer, heat-set the paint following the manufacturer's recommendations.

ALL-OVER GEOMETRIC NAPKINS

PATTERN STYLE: Geometric

PATTERN REPEAT:
Straight and Brick

TECHNIQUE: Stamping

Every printing motif can be used in a variety of ways. I made this set of napkins using the same stamping blocks that I used on the Geometric Striped Tablecloth (page 49). I varied the repeat styles but kept the color of base fabric and printing ink the same. The motifs can be staggered up and down or across. This is a good project with which to explore different kinds of repeats—straight, drop, or brick (see "Pattern Repeats" on page 8). The stamps could also be printed randomly with a lot or a little space in between. Once you begin playing with different repeats, you will quickly learn that there are so many possibilities. If you are like me, you will find it is hard to stop.

SUPPLIES

FOR THE STAMPS

Templates
(see pages 166–70)

Craft foam with adhesive backing

1-inch-thick foam building insulation

Scissors

Tape

Utility knife

FOR THE NAPKINS

6 handmade or store-bought 18-inch linen napkins (see note)

Steam iron

Drop cloth

Latex paint (see note)

Golden GAC 900 Fabric Painting Medium

Versatex Fixer, optional

½-inch and 1-inch foam brushes

Deli containers for holding paint

Table for printing

Fabric and craft scissors

Auto-fade fabric marker (optional)

NOTE: For this project, I used latex house paint mixed with fabric medium to print the motifs. It is opaque and sits nicely on top of the linen fabric. I used dark brown paint. I made my own linen napkins out of 1 yard of 54-inch linen fabric. See "Basic Technique: Making Napkins" on page 37 for how to make your own napkins.

1. Prewash your napkins and dry them in the dryer. Remove them before they are completely dry so the wrinkles do not set. Iron the napkins.

2. Prepare the stamps. Make stamps using the templates for the hexagon, open circle, split circle, little squares, large triangle, and diamond (see "Basic Technique: Making Stamps" on page 33).

3. Cover your work surface with a drop cloth.

4. Mix the latex paint with the fabric medium, following the manufacturer's directions. You will not need a lot of paint. If you run out, you can mix more. I begin by mixing 1 tablespoon of paint with 1 tablespoon of fabric medium. Add the Versatex Fixer if you are using it.

5. Mark the center of the napkin both vertically and horizontally. To do this, fold the napkin wrong sides together and with your fingers or an iron press the center crease. Next, fold the napkin in half again, matching the hemmed edges and forming a center fold. Press this crease with your fingers or an iron. Open the napkin and lay it flat. The creases form a horizontal and vertical guide for the stamping process. Alternately, you can use an auto-fade fabric marker and a graph ruler to mark the horizontal and vertical center points.

6. Use a foam brush to apply paint to the stamp. Try a few sample stamps on scrap fabric to get the feeling of the pressure needed. Press the stamp firmly onto the fabric. (See "Basic Technique: Making Stamps" on page 33.)

7. To print the napkins, begin at the center horizontal fold line and print the stamps across the fabric. The motifs can be printed on both sides of the fold or centered on the fold. Try to keep the spacing equal between each stamp. For the next row of stamps, print the stamps above the horizontal fold line. Continue until the entire napkin is covered with stamps. At the borders of the napkins, some of the motifs will be partial motifs. Alternately, you can stop printing and have full motifs and plain edges (see the

Diamond Napkin). Here is how I spaced each of the patterns:

- **HEXAGON (BRICK REPEAT)**—Print the first hexagon motif over the center of the vertical fold, placing a tip of the hexagon along the horizontal fold. Print a hexagon using the same horizontal fold placement ¼ inch away from the center motif on both sides. Print partial hexagons to finish the row. The next row of hexagons should be printed in the open space created by the first row. Spacing should be ¼ inch away, and a point should face down toward the first row of motifs. Continue printing the pattern as established, filling up the entire napkin. There will be partial hexagons at all 4 edges.

- **DIAMOND (STRAIGHT REPEAT)**— Print the first motif directly in the middle of the napkin over the intersection of the 2 folds. Print 4 diamonds to the right and left of the center diamond using the horizontal fold as a guide for placement. The side points of each diamond motif should touch each other. Print 2 more rows of diamonds, 1 row above and 1 row below the center row. The points should just touch each other.

- **OPEN CIRCLE (STRAIGHT REPEAT)**— Print the first motif directly in the middle of the napkin over the intersection of the 2 folds. Print a circle on both sides of the center motif ¼ inch away from the first. Finish the row

Hexagon
(brick repeat)

with 1 half circle at the edge of the napkin. Print 1 row of circles directly above and below the center row. Finish with a partial row of circles directly above and below the last rows.

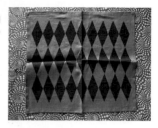

Diamond
(straight repeat)

- **SPLIT CIRCLE (STRAIGHT REPEAT)**— Print the first motif directly in the middle of the napkin over the intersection of the 2 folds. Print a circle on both sides of the center motif ¼ inch away from the first. Print 1 row of circles ¼ inch directly above and below the center row.

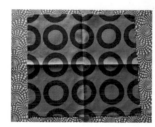

Open circle
(straight repeat)

- **LITTLE SQUARES (STRAIGHT REPEAT)**—Begin stamping just below the horizontal fold, printing 4 motifs ¼ inch apart. Print 3 more rows of motifs ¼ to ½ inch above and below the first row to fill the napkin.

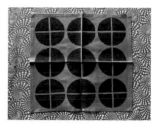

Split circle
(straight repeat)

- **TRIANGLE (STRAIGHT REPEAT)**— Begin with the triangle point centered and facing down; print 4 stamps across. End with a small bit of the triangle stamp at each side. Rotate the stamp so the triangle point faces up. Print 3 full triangles in the open space, ½ inch from the first row of triangles. Print 2 partial triangles on each side. Continue stamping the pattern as established, filling up the entire napkin.

Little squares
(straight repeat)

8. If you did not use the Versatex Fixer, heat-set the paint following the manufacturer's recommendations.

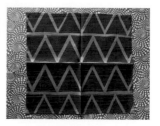

Triangle
(straight repeat)

CIRCLE AND DOTS PLATES

> **PATTERN STYLE:** Geometric
> **PATTERN REPEAT:** Random
> **TECHNIQUE:** Ceramics

I have a serious addiction to collecting handmade and antique ceramics. I love colorful ceramics decorated with bright colors, flowers, and small patterns almost as much as I love serving with, eating off of, and decorating with them. Many years ago, I took a nighttime adult education class to learn to throw pots on a potter's wheel in an effort to curb my ceramic buying addiction. That class started me on a very rewarding and creative journey of building and decorating handmade ceramics. I still buy the odd pot on occasion, but now my focus is on making and decorating my own ceramics.

I have my own pottery studio and ceramic kiln, but you'll need access to a pottery studio that's open to the public to complete this project. The studio will supply you with undecorated bisqueware plates and underglaze for decoration. They will then add a gloss glaze when firing your plates.

For this set of plates, I chose a circle theme that is approachable and easy for a beginner to copy. It is amazing how many variations you can make on circles and dots—it really is endless. Having plates of your own design to use on your kitchen table is a way to make your nest totally your own.

SUPPLIES

Undecorated ceramic bisqueware plates	Round artist's brushes in various sizes
Number 2 pencil	Newspaper to protect table
Underglaze for painting designs (see note)	Water for rinsing brush
	Gloss glaze (see note)

NOTE: If you are using a pottery studio that's open to the public to make this project, you'll likely need to work with the glazes they have. I used Amazo LUG-21 Medium Blue. Request that the studio apply a gloss glaze before firing to make the plates washable and food safe.

1. Wipe the plates with a damp, clean cloth so they are clean and free of any dust and dirt.

2. With a pencil, sketch out your design ideas on a piece of paper (see some ideas below). Once you are happy with them, use the pencil to transfer the ideas to the plates. The pencil marks will burn off in the kiln. The circles and dots are not very difficult to paint so you may be able to skip the step of drawing on the plates.

3. Using artist's brushes and underglazes, paint the designs of your choice on each plate. Let the underglaze dry.

4. Apply the gloss glaze and fire your plates to make them food safe.

DESIGN IDEAS FOR CIRCLE AND DOT VARIATIONS

- very small pinhead-size dots randomly placed and interspersed with ¼-inch dots
- circles painted with a ¼-inch border and open in the center
- solid dots ½ inch to 1 inch in diameter randomly placed
- concentric circle painted with ¼-inch lines placed slightly off center
- open circles painted with a ¼-inch border; centers and outer rims of the circles decorated with varying sizes of dots
- open circles painted with a ¼-inch border randomly spaced; solid circles painted inside and small dots randomly placed

HEXAGON CROCHET AFGHAN

PATTERN STYLE: Geometric
PATTERN REPEAT: Half Drop
TECHNIQUE: Crochet

Western Massachusetts has cold, long winters. I keep woolen throws and crocheted afghans on every piece of furniture, including the daybed in the kitchen. They are indispensable in the morning and the evening while we wait for the furnace and woodstove to heat up. My family fights over who gets to use the crocheted afghans. There is something so cozy about these blankets—the fabric has a bit of openness to it and it molds around your body to keep you really warm.

I have been fascinated by the possibilities of hexagons—in quilts, printing (see the "All-Over Geometric Napkins" project on page 52), and now crochet. They are easy to make and quite addicting. For this project, I wanted a modern look for my afghan, so I made the hexagons in only two colors. The complementary shades of purple and green look gorgeous together.

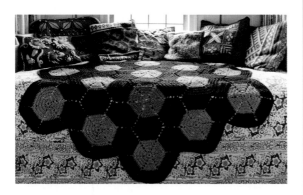

SUPPLIES

Worsted-weight wool in Color A (green), 6 balls (50 grams = 93 yards)—approximately 560 yards total

Worsted-weight wool in Color B (purple), 14 balls (50 grams = 93 yards)—approximately 1,400 yards total

Crochet hook in size I

Tapestry needle

STITCH ABBREVIATIONS

ch—chain

dc—double crochet

sp—space

sl st—slip stitch

FINISHED SIZE: Each hexagon measures approximately 11 inches across; the finished blanket is 66 inches long × 55 inches wide.

FOUNDATION RING: Using Color A, ch 6 and join with a sl st to form a ring.

ROUND 1: Ch4 (counts as 1 dc), [1 dc into ring, ch1] 11 times, join with a sl st into 3rd ch of ch4—(12 spaced dc).

ROUND 2: Ch3 (counts as 1 dc), 2 dc into next ch 1 sp, 1 dc into next dc, ch2, *1 dc into next dc, 2 dc into next ch1 sp, 1 dc into next dc, ch 2; rep from * 4 times, join with sl st to 3rd ch of ch 3.

ROUND 3: Ch3, 1 dc into same place, 1 dc into each of next 2 dc, 2 dc into next dc, ch2, *2dc into next dc, 1 dc into each of next 2 dc, 2 dc into next dc, ch2; rep from * 4 times, join with a sl st to 3rd ch of ch3.

ROUND 4: Ch3, 1 dc into same place, 1 dc into each of next 4 dc, 2 dc into next dc, ch 2, *2 dc into next dc, 1 dc into each of next 4 dc, 2 dc into next dc, ch2; rep from * 4 times, join with a sl st to 3rd ch of ch 3.

ROUND 5: Ch3, 1 dc into same place, 1 dc into each of next 6 dc, 2 dc into next dc, ch 2, *2 dc into next dc, 1 dc into each of next 6 dc, 2 dc into next dc, ch2; rep from * 4 times, join with a sl st to 3rd ch of ch 3.

Change to Color B for remainder of hexagon.

ROUND 6: With B, ch3, 1 dc into same place, 1 dc into each of next 8 dc, 2 dc into next dc, ch 2, *2 dc into next dc, 1 dc into each of next 8 dc, 2 dc into next dc, ch2; rep from * 4 times, join with a sl st to 3rd ch of ch 3.

ROUND 7: Ch3, 1 dc into same place, 1 dc into each of next 10 dc, 2 dc into next dc, ch 2, *2 dc into next dc, 1 dc into each of next 10 dc, 2 dc into next dc, ch2; rep from * 4 times, join with a sl st to 3rd ch of ch 3.

ROUND 8: Ch3, 1 dc into same place, 1 dc into each of next 12 dc, 2 dc into next dc, ch 2, *2 dc into next dc, 1 dc into each of next 12 dc, 2 dc into next dc, ch2; rep from * 4 times, join with a sl st to 3rd ch of ch 3.

ROUND 9: Ch3, 1 dc into same place, 1 dc into each of next 14 dc, 2 dc into next dc, ch 2, *2 dc into next dc, 1 dc into each of next 14 dc, 2 dc into next dc, ch2; rep from * 4 times, join with a sl st to 3rd ch of ch 3.

Make 24 hexagons.

Sew the hexagons together using a whip stitch with the darker color yarn. See the illustration for placement. You will have rows of hexagons as follows: 4 hexagons across, 5 hexagons across, 6 hexagons across, 5 hexagons across, 4 hexagons across.

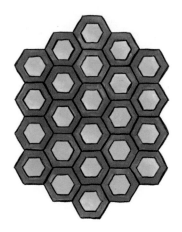

PLAID WALL TREATMENT

> **PATTERN STYLE:** Geometric
> **PATTERN REPEAT:** Straight
> **TECHNIQUE:** Masking and painting

SUPPLIES

Latex paint in a variety of colors (see note)

Painter's blue masking tape—1 inch wide

Yardstick

Builder's level

Pencil

Rags

Water

Deli containers for mixing paint

Stippling brush, dauber, or stiff brush

NOTE: For this project I used 5 colors: orange, blue, moss green, medium brown, and dark purple.

I love a mix of patterns in a room. I think it makes a space look more interesting and gives a homey feeling. After I painted the flora and fauna mural above the chair rail in the dining room, I decided to treat the space under the chair rail with a plaid design. In the decorating trade, this is called pattern on pattern. The graphic plaid design is a visual contrast to the swirling flowers and vines on the main part of the walls.

Creating a plaid wall treatment isn't too hard—as long as you have patience and don't mind doing a lot of measuring and taping. The basic idea behind creating this design is that you apply blue painter's tape vertically to sections that will not be painted. The tape acts as a resist—similar to the wax that is used to create designs in batik. Once the tape is removed, there will be a stripe on the wall. By then applying tape horizontally, as I have done in the dining room, a plaid design is created. I also employed some decorative paint techniques—color washing, mottling, and mixing of colors on the wall—to make my plaid wall treatment even more interesting.

1. Colorwash the walls to create the background for the plaid design. I did 3 layers of color. I began by painting the wall orange as the base coat. I then washed the wall with a layer of blue. The top coat is the most important color. It will give the wall its overall color. I chose a mossy green. (See "Basic Technique: Colorwashing" on page 28 for detailed instructions on colorwashing walls.)

2. Determine the spacing for the stripes. (See Figure 1.) My stripes were 3¾ inches wide. Begin at a corner. For each stripe, hold the level vertically and use a pencil to lightly draw a straight line up the entire wall. Draw these lines all the way around the room, 3¾ inches apart.

   Place 1-inch-wide tape along the pencil line, making sure the pencil line will be painted over. Press firmly along the edge of the tape so the paint will not seep under. Move to the next line and finish taping off the stripe. Continue to tape off every other stripe so that the stripes between will be open so you can cover them with paint.

Mix the paint and water in a deli container until it is the consistency of heavy cream. Using medium brown latex paint and a towel, colorwash each stripe section. Let the paint dry. Remove the tape. Do not leave the tape on too long or it could pull off the color underneath. You will have wide vertical stripes.

3. For the wide horizontal bands of color, repeat steps 2 and 3, placing the tape horizontally along the wall at the proper heights. (See Figure 2.) Use the level, a yardstick for measuring, and a pencil for marking. Run the tape horizontally across the wall. My horizontal stripes were 4 inches tall and were spaced equally in the chair rail space. The green (unpainted) stripes were 3¾ inches wide.

4. With a stippling brush, dauber, or stiff brush, use a quick pouncing motion to paint between the rows of tape. To make a mottled stripe as shown, dip the brush into 2 colors (I used mossy green and purple). Pounce the brush randomly to create a mottled stripe. Repeat until all horizontal stripes are complete. Let the paint dry. Remove the tape.

5. The central thin plaid lines were made with orange paint in the center of each wide brown stripe. (See Figure 3.) Draw 2 vertical lines 1 inch apart in the center of the first vertical stripe. Place the 1-inch tape along the outside of each line to create a 1-inch stripe in the center of the first wide vertical stripe. Using a stippling brush, dauber, or stiff brush, paint the stripes. I used orange paint and applied the paint thinly so that the other layers below would show through slightly. Let the paint dry. Remove the tape.

6. Repeat step 5, placing the tape horizontally across the 2 mottled wide stripes to create an orange plaid design. Using a stippling brush, dauber, or stiff brush, paint the horizontal stripes. Let the paint dry. Remove the tape.

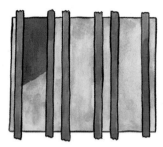

Figure 1

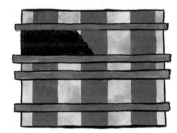

Figure 2

Figure 3

SCRAPBOOK COASTERS

PATTERN STYLE: Organic
PATTERN REPEAT: Random
TECHNIQUE: Digital Printing

I have several sets of coasters that I use in every room in our home to protect wood surfaces from drippy glasses. I used one of my favorite world textiles as the basis for this quick-to-make set of coasters. I laid the fabric on the floor and took a photo of it. Using my computer, I manipulated the image with filters to make it look bright and graphic. You could photograph any fabric or piece of artwork, such as a child's drawing you have in your home, patterned gift wrapping, or scrapbooking paper.

SUPPLIES

Photo of hand-embroidered fabric or scrapbooking paper

Camera

Computer

Photo-editing program such as Photoshop or PicMonkey (available free online)

Laser printer

Card stock for printing

Cork coasters available from craft stores

Glue

Polyurethane

Foam paintbrush

Scissors or X-Acto knife

1. Lay the fabric on the floor or a table and take a photo. Don't worry if it isn't the best. You will manipulate it using a computer.

2. Bring the image into a photo-editing program and size it to fit a standard piece of paper. You can make 4 coasters out of a letter-size print. Using filters in the photo-editing program, manipulate the image to your liking. I changed the contrast and brightness on my photo and used the Posterize filter in Photoshop. A similar effect is possible in PicMonkey (a free photo-editing program) using the Boost filter.

3. Print the photo on card stock using a laser printer. (Ink-jet prints will run when covered with liquid.) If you do not have access to a laser printer, have it printed at a copy center. Alternately use wrapping or scrapbooking paper.

4. Trace the cork shapes on the paper. Using scissors or an X-Acto knife, cut out the shapes.

5. Using a craft brush and glue, attach the paper to the cork backs. Spread the glue evenly and all the way to the edge so the piece will lie flat. Let the glue dry.

6. Using polyurethane and a foam brush, paint 3 layers of clear finish, letting it dry between each coat.

CHAPTER TWO

LIVING ROOM
AND
LIBRARY

LAYERS OF PATTERN GIVE A WARM AND INVITING FEELING TO OUR LIVING ROOM. ONCE USED AS THE CENTRAL KITCHEN AND LIVING SPACE WHEN THE FARMHOUSE WAS BUILT IN 1751, THE LIVING ROOM STILL FEATURES A MASSIVE WORKING BRICK FIREPLACE. WE USE THIS LARGE SPACE FOR FAMILY GATHERINGS AND as a space to relax on a winter day in front of a warm fire. The walls are painted in mottled and streaky shades of gold and chartreuse applied using decorative painting techniques. They serve as a solid backdrop for the patterned textiles that cover the sofa, chairs, and tables. Fringed wool plaid blankets and embroidered floral throws are scattered throughout the space to add warmth—for both a visual and a functional purpose. The west wall is covered with bookcases and small closets painted in a vibrant shade of bright green. The bookcases are overfilled with art, design, and textile books and their colorful spines add random pattern to the room. Along the edges of the gold walls, I stamped a paisley motif to add more pattern to the room. The hallway leading upstairs is painted in a colorwashed turquoise shade and is decorated with a hand-stamped floral and stripe design. Collections of objects—Staffordshire ceramics, cloisonné vases, and more books—are scattered throughout the room. They add layers of interest and initiate conversations. On the floor, a smattering of different floral and geometric patterned rugs helps complete the casual elegance.

Just off the living room, an olive green door leads into the library. Again, a hearth is central to the use of the library. My family and I gather every evening around the wood stove in the tiny room during the winter months. Hand-painted ceramic tiles in a riot of bright colors on the fireplace surround add to the eclectic mix of patterns that abound in the library. Above the dark wood mantelpiece, an odd collection of colorful ceramics increases the visual clutter. One wall is covered with a charcoal gray bookcase overflowing with more books. Hand-stitched textiles from India and Uzbekistan decorate the bookcase, the mantel, and the window frames. A much-used and worn red jacquard sofa proves that visible age gives a well-loved feeling to a space. On the walls, I painted wallpaper and a mural to add a splash of color and more pattern. A large collection of framed antique prints featuring sheep bring our farming occupation into the decoration of the room. My goal when designing the space was to have a room that was so comfortable that it would feel as if time were standing still and as if our family has lived here for generations. The mix of vibrant and busy patterns certainly helped to accomplish that feeling.

COMPASS PRINTED AND EMBROIDERED PILLOW

In our area, we are lucky to have many historic homes like ours to look at and learn from. Historic Deerfield is a colonial village where guests can tour antique, restored homes and see how colonists lived. A wealth of old things—furniture, silver, ceramics, fabrics, clothing, and more—finds a home in collections in historic Deerfield and other local museums. I frequently visit them looking for inspiration for my textile designs and ceramics.

I stumbled upon a Polychrome Hadley Chest at the Memorial Hall Museum in Deerfield. It was made in 1715 and was highly decorated with painted motifs that were made using a compass. Only four of these chests are known to exist in the world. I was struck by how contemporary the motifs looked. It is hard to believe the craftsperson had such precision of paint and carving considering the hardships they were working under. I couldn't stop thinking about the chests. I designed this pillow as an ode to the Hadley chest makers. My interpretation of the motifs is printed and embroidered. The slow process of the embroidered stitch that outlines the motifs seems a fitting way to connect with these remarkable artists and their work.

SUPPLIES

FOR THE STAMPS

Templates (see page 171)

Craft foam with adhesive backing

1-inch-thick foam building insulation

Acrylic mount

Scissors

Tape

Utility knife

FOR THE PILLOW

⅝ yard of linen fabric in celery

⅝ yard of backing fabric in a colorful pattern

Steam iron

Drop cloth

Jacquard Textile Colors fabric paint in goldenrod and orange

Versatex Fixer, optional

½-inch and 1-inch foam brushes

Deli container for holding paint

Table for printing

Fabric and craft scissors

Crewel wool thread: 1 skein each in royal blue and turquoise

Sewing machine

18-inch down pillow insert

1. Prewash the fabric and hang it to dry. Iron it with a steam iron to smooth out the wrinkles. Cut the linen to measure 19 × 19 inches. Cut the backing fabric following the instructions (see "Basic Technique: Making an Easy Throw Pillow" on page 38).

2. Using the templates and following the instructions, assemble the foam stamps (see "Basic Technique: Making Stamps" on page 33). Use builder's foam to mount the circle and acrylic to mount the flower.

3. Cover a table with a drop cloth to protect the printing surface.

4. To determine the center of the fabric, fold it in half so that 2 raw edges meet. Then fold it in half again so the opposite 2 raw edges meet. With your fingers or an iron, press the folds. This crease makes a guide to follow when printing.

5. Follow the directions for printing with foam stamps (see "Stamping Tips" on page 32). Coat the stamp with goldenrod fabric paint. Beginning at the center fold and using the circle stamp, print the first circle with its center directly in the center of the fabric. Print 1 circle on each side of the center circle, approximately ¾ inches away, centering it on the horizontal fold. Print 2 circles, approximately ¼ inch away from the top of the first row of circles, centering them between the 2 circles below them. This is called a brick repeat. Repeat with 2 circles below the first row.

6. Print the 6-petal flower motif in the center of each circle in orange fabric paint, lining up the outside of the flower with the outside edge of each circle.

7. Let the paint dry. If you did not use Versatex Fixer, heat-set the paint according to the manufacturer's directions.

8. Add the embroidery. Using a single strand of blue thread, work an outline stitch around each circle placing the stitches on the edge of the circle. Using a single strand of turquoise thread, work an outline stitch around each petal.

9. To make the pillowcase, follow the instructions for a flap back pillow. (See "Basic Technique: Making an Easy Throw Pillow" on page 38.)

OUTLINE STITCH

1. Come up at A at the beginning of the line. Take a backwards stitch from B to C (halfway between A and B), and pull the needle through, keeping the thread above the line of stitching.

2. Take a stitch from D to B, keeping the thread above the line of stitching. You will see that a heavy line of stitching develops as this new stitch overlaps the previous stitch. Make sure the thread always stays on the same side of the line. To end, go down at E. When working around a curve, the threads sometimes fall down on the shape. To remedy this, make tiny stitches.

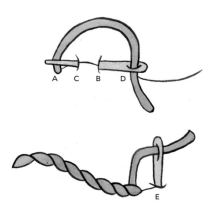

BLOOMSBURY-INSPIRED PAINTED TABLETOP

> **PATTERN STYLE:** Geometric
> **PATTERN REPEAT:** Straight
> **TECHNIQUE:** Painting

Many years ago, I purchased this small round oak table in a secondhand shop in Lowell, Massachusetts, for five dollars. It has sat next to a couch in the living room and has been covered with a rotating selection of patterned textiles because the paint was in bad shape. My plan has always been to paint it decoratively, but somehow I never got around to it until now. Inspired by the hand-painted furniture done by the Bloomsbury artists, I did my own take.

Painting furniture is a fantastic way to add your own style to your home. Look for solid wood furniture that might not be appealing in its current state. You can frequently pick it up very inexpensively at estate auctions and thrift stores. Don't feel you have to be an artist to do a project like this. It is quite easy once you begin. I sketched out a rough idea on paper using geometric shapes to create the motifs. I used a ruler, plate, and large platter to pencil in my design idea on the table. Once I had the main motifs painted in different colors, I began decorating them with little flourishes like dashes, crosses, dots, finger smears, and lines to add detail. On the base of the table, I painted different colors following the carving of the wood. If you are worried about the painted design being damaged, cover it with a couple coats of polyurethane to seal the paint.

SUPPLIES

Round table to paint	Pencil
2-inch paintbrush	Ruler
Artist's paintbrushes in various sizes	Household items to trace (see note)
Latex paint in semi-gloss finish in various colors	Stain and rag, optional
Sketchbook for ideas	Polyurethane, optional

NOTE: Look around your home for household items that are interesting shapes. Trace them to create designs on the table. A plate (circle), coaster (square), a pack of cards (rectangle with rounded corners), jar (circle), platter (oval), and more will give you plenty of templates to make your design.

1. Sand the table to remove loose bits of finish and prepare it for painting. Wash it to remove any dirt and odd bits. Let the table dry.

2. Paint the table with your chosen base coat. I used turquoise.

3. Draw some ideas in your sketchbook. Start with a round circle or the shape of your table. Draw circles and other geometric shapes to plan your design. A good way to begin is to dissect the table shape by dividing it in halves, quarters, sixths, or eighths. Draw repeating shapes in the different sections. Once you begin doing this, you will see all the infinite possibilities that await you. Think about household objects that you might be able to trace and use as part of your design.

4. Once you come up with a design you like, transfer it to the table following your sketch. Use a pencil, ruler, and other household items to map out your design. To make the semi-circles on the outer edge of the table, I used the rim of a platter. To make the petal shape,

I folded a piece of heavy paper in half and cut a petal shape. I traced around the shapes, rotating their positions in each section.

5. Fill in the shapes with paint. Let each section dry. Add a second coat if you want. I like the color below to show through a bit to add an artistic transparent effect.

6. Once you are happy with your shapes, decorate them with squiggles, lines, dots, and dashes. Use your fingertips to make ovals and round dots. A small circle cut from a sponge will make a mottled circle stamp. The edge of a foam brush makes a good dash. Artist's brushes work for crosses and dotted lines.

7. If you want to give the table an aged look, rub it with a thin coat of stain or thinned-down latex paint using a rag. Let the paint dry.

8. Apply 2 coats of polyurethane to protect your design.

CHARLESTON FARMHOUSE AND THE BLOOMSBURY GROUP

Back in the early 1990s, my friend Sally sent me a book titled *Bloomsbury: Its Artists, Authors and Designers.* She knew I would like it as it was about the artists known as the Bloomsbury Group. Duncan Grant, Vanessa Bell, Clive Bell, Roger Fry, Vanessa's sister Virginia Woolf, and many more bohemian artists, writers, and thinkers lived in the early part of the twentieth century in the Bloomsbury neighborhood of London—hence the name. In 1916 during the First World War, Duncan, Clive, Vanessa, and Virginia moved to Sussex to escape London. Vanessa found a farmhouse to rent, called Charleston, and lived there with Clive, Duncan, and their children—Vanessa had children with both Clive and Duncan. At Charleston, they hand-painted the entire house—furniture, walls, woodwork, ceramics, and more with their floral, geometric, and quirky designs. They created lines of fabric for fabric manufacturers and even ceramics for Clarice Cliff and Wedgewood. Vanessa and Clive's son, Quentin Bell, made pottery in a studio at Charleston for many years.

Vanessa and Duncan were primarily oil painters and their art is in museums and collections all over the world. Vanessa passed away in 1961. Duncan Grant lived at Charleston until he died in 1978. A Trust was formed, and over several years, the patterned and painted farmhouse was restored. It opened to the public in 1986. Charleston has become a mecca for creative people. Sally and I visited there together in 1999, just after my husband Mark and I had purchased our farmhouse. To say that I was inspired by all the colorful paintings, fabrics, rugs, walls, needlework, interior decoration, ceramics, and the creative spirit of the artists and writers of Bloomsbury and Charleston would be an understatement.

KNITTED PILLOW

For years, I worked as the creative director for a yarn company. One of the most enjoyable parts of my job was to come up with hand-knitting designs to help sell our yarn. After many years of designing sweaters, I grew tired of churning out garment after garment. I was becoming more and more interested in interior decorating. Referencing the beautiful hand-stitched needlepoint pillows that I saw in many handmade interiors, I set about designing knitting charts to mimic the stitched designs. I knit them up, photographed them, and wrote the instructions. They were a big success, and I was hooked.

Over the years, I have knit many colorful pillows for our home. Knit pillows are such a lovely accent—something about the knit fabric speaks warmth and love and comfort. Here is a new design that you can make for your home. After the pillow is knit, embroider chain stitches and French knots to add even more color.

SUPPLIES

Worsted-weight wool yarn in 4 colors: 180 yards each of Color A (chartreuse) and Color B (raspberry) and 20 yards each of Color C (red), and Color D (pink)

Knitting needles: one 16-inch circular needle in size US 5

Stitch markers

Blunt tapestry needle

14-inch down pillow insert

½ yard of backing fabric

Sewing needle and matching thread

Sewing machine

T-pins for blocking

GAUGE: 20 stitches and 22 rounds = 4 inches (10 cm) in stockinette stitch colorwork

NOTE: The pillow front is knit in the round with steek stitches at the beginning and end of the round. During finishing, the tube is cut to form a flat pillow front and the mitered edge trim is added. If you prefer, knit the pillow back and forth on circular needles. You will not need to cut the fabric.

When working in the round, read all chart rows from right to left as RS rows. If working back and forth, read all RS rows (odd-numbered rows) from right to left and all WS rows (even-numbered rows) from left to right.

STITCH GUIDE

Stockinette Stitch in the Round (St st):

Knit all stitches every round.

Stockinette Stitch Back and Forth (St st):

Row 1: Knit all sts.

Row 2: Purl all sts.

Reverse Stockinette Stitch Ridge (RSSR; worked in the round for border)

Rnd 1: Knit.

Rnds 2 and 3: Purl.

Repeat these three rounds for pattern.

STITCH ABBREVIATIONS

K—knit

St(s)—stitch(es)

Rnd—round

Rem—remaining

M—make

St st—Stockinette Stitch

RSSR—Reverse Stockinette Stitch

1. Knit the pillow front. Using Color A, cast on 79 sts. Join in the round, taking care not to twist any stitches. Establish steeks and Rnd 1 of chart with Colors A and B as follows: K3 steek sts, place marker, work 24-st chart pattern 3 times over next 72 sts, then work stitch 25, place marker, k3 steek sts—73 sts in pattern from chart; 3 steek sts at each end of rnd. Using Colors A and B, work Rnds 1 to 24

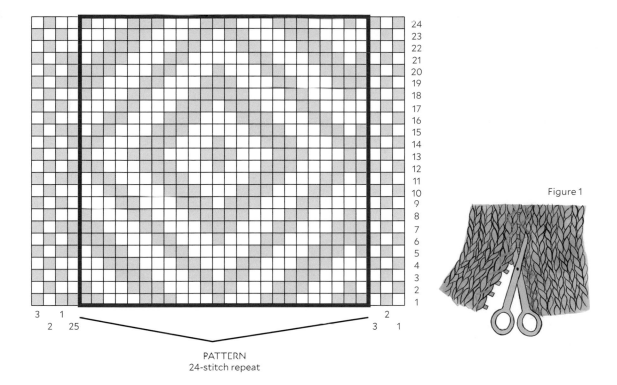

Figure 1

	24
	23
	22
	21
	20
	19
	18
	17
	16
	15
	14
	13
	12
	11
	10
	9
	8
	7
	6
	5
	4
	3
	2
	1

3 1
2 25   3 1
                                          2

PATTERN
24-stitch repeat

of the chart 3 times. Work Rnd 1 again. Bind off all sts with Color A.

2. Secure and cut the steek. Using a sewing machine set to zigzag stitch, or a very small backstitch stitch if sewing by hand, sew down the middle of the 2 center steek stitches. Carefully cut the pillow tube open in between the 2 rows of zigzag stitch. (See Figure 1.)

3. Knit the mitered edge. Using Color C, and with RS facing, *pick up and knit 65 sts along the CO or BO edge of the pattern section (do not pick up along steek sts), place marker, pick up 1 st in the corner, place marker, pick up and knit 48 sts at next edge between the pattern and steek sts, place marker, pick up 1 st in the corner, place marker; rep from * for rem 2 sides—230 sts. This pick-up rnd counts as Rnd 1 of first Reverse Stockinette Stitch Ridge (RSSR).

ROUND 2: With Color C, *increase 1 st by placing a backward loop on the needle (referred to as M1), purl to marker, M1, slip marker, k1 (corner st), slip marker; rep from * 3 more times—8 sts increased; 238 sts total.

ROUND 3: Purl one rnd, knitting each marked corner st—first RSSR completed.

Change to Color D and work 3 rnds of second RSSR, knitting the corner sts every rnd, and increasing 8 sts in Rnds 1 and 3—254 sts. Change to Color D and work Rnds 1 to 3 of third RSSR, knitting the corner sts as before, and increasing 8 sts in Rnd 2 only—262 sts.

Change to Color C and work another RSSR. Repeat miter pattern and at corners on Rnds 1 and 3, increasing 2 sts at each corner every other round—278 sts. With Color C, bind off all sts firmly in knit st.

4. Add the embroidery referring to the photo. At the inside of each middle-sized diamond, work in chain stitch in Color D. At the center of each small diamond, work a French knot in Color C.

5. Block the pillow top. Using a spray bottle, thoroughly mist the pillow top with warm water and work the water into the knitted fabric. Using large T-pins, pin out the fabric on a flat padded surface. Using a steam iron held 2 inches away from the fabric, steam lightly. Avoid touching the pillow with the iron or the fabric may become flattened or scorched. Allow the fabric to dry. Alternately, hand wash the pillow in cold water, cold rinse, and lay it flat to dry. Weave in the ends.

6. Assemble the pillow. Cut the backing fabric 1 inch wider and longer than the blocked pillow top including the mitered trim. Turn the edges ½ inch to the wrong side on all 4 sides and press in place. Hand stitch the backing to the WS of the pillow top around 3 sides. Insert the pillow form. Sew the last side closed.

CHAIN STITCH

1. Come up at A. Take a stitch from B to C, but do not pull the needle through. Wrap the thread under the needle at C. Pull the needle through and a loop will form on top of the fabric. Continue by inserting your needle at D (inside the loop), then come up at E, again wrapping the yarn under the needle before you pull the needle through.

2. To end, insert your needle at F just outside the loop and pull to the back side to finish the stitch.

FRENCH KNOT

1. Come up at A. With your left hand (right hand, for lefties), wrap the thread twice around the needle.

2. Rotate the needle toward the fabric, and insert the needle at B while tightly pulling on the wraps. Pull the needle to the back, and a knot will form on the surface.

PAISLEY HAND-PRINTED UPHOLSTERED CHAIR

> **PATTERN STYLE:** Organic
> **PATTERN REPEAT:** Straight
> **TECHNIQUE:** Stamping

This is my chair. It is where I sit almost every evening in our cozy library. I knit or sew or read in it. Like much of our furniture, it came from a secondhand store, and I can imagine it was someone else's favorite chair before me. It is sturdy and has a squishy down cushion. When I found it, I had it reupholstered in a buffalo check fabric. Sadly, the fabric wore out and so it was time to re-cover it once again.

I chose my favorite paisley motif for the design and decided to print the fabric myself. I used the wrong side of a thick twill weave cotton fabric. I made the stamp out of craft foam. Because I wanted to print yardage, I decided to keep the pattern simple and oriented the paisley motif only one way—leaning to the right. It took quite a while to stamp all the fabric I needed, but I worked on it over several days. If you don't have the time or energy to print enough yardage to cover a chair, start with fabric for small cushions. I love the wonky hand-printed quality of the stamping and think it adds an artistic vibe to my favorite chair.

The paisley motif has been a favorite of mine. To me, the motif has always spoken of a celebration of life. Its organic shape and often layered multi-motif and multi-colored presentation are hard to resist.

The paisley motif has a very rich and long history in textiles of the world. In ancient Persia, the paisley motif is called a "boteh." In India, the paisley motif is often embroidered onto shawls. Slowly, the motif was imported to Western Europe and it became all the rage. The word "paisley" comes from Paisley, a town in Scotland where jacquard looms were used to produce machine-woven shawls in the mid-1800s onward. The fabric house Liberty of London has been known for its different versions of the paisley motif that have been used in interior and fashion design since the late 1800s. The motif's popularity ebbs and flows but in my world, it is always in fashion. When it became time for my chair to be reupholstered, I turned to the paisley motif.

SUPPLIES

FOR THE STAMP

Template (see page 172)

Craft foam with adhesive backing

1-inch-thick foam building insulation

Scissors

Tape

Utility knife

FOR THE FABRIC

Enough yardage to cover a chair (see note)

Steam iron

Drop cloth

Latex paint in olive green and red

Golden GAC 900 Fabric Painting Medium

Versatex Fixer, optional

½-inch and 1-inch foam brushes

Deli container for holding paint

Table for printing

Fabric and craft scissors

NOTE: Although I could have taught myself to upholster my chair, I decided to hire an upholsterer since I wanted an excellent job and needed to save time. Talk to your upholsterer about the width of the fabric and number of yards you need to print. For my chair, it wasn't necessary for me to print the entire width of the fabric because a smaller width was needed. This can save you some time. For fun, I chose 3 different color fabrics to print—red, khaki, and gold.

1. Following the instructions, assemble the foam stamp (see "Basic Technique: Making Stamps" on page 33).

2. Cover the printing surface with the drop cloth. Lay out the fabric on top and iron it to remove wrinkles.

3. Dilute the latex paint with the fabric medium as instructed by the manufacturer. If you like, use Versatex Fixer in your paint so that heat-setting will not be necessary.

4. To determine my pattern spacing, I made small paper guides to space the paisley motif vertically. To space the rows of paisleys, I used a long piece of wooden molding as a guide.

5. Follow directions for printing with foam stamps (see "Stamping Tips" on page 32). Test your stamping pattern on a piece of scrap fabric to practice the spacing. Print rows and rows of paisleys. I tried to place them exactly above the last row, although I wasn't always accurate.

6. Let the paint dry. If you did not use Versatex Fixer, heat-set the paint according to the manufacturer's directions.

7. Give the fabric to an upholsterer to cover the chair.

COLORFUL TILE FIREPLACE SURROUND

> **PATTERN STYLE:**
> Assorted (each tile is different)
> **PATTERN REPEAT:** Random
> **TECHNIQUE:** Ceramics and Tiling

I visit a lot of historic house museums. Many of them were built in the Victorian era in the late 1800s. At that time, fireplaces were used every day and were also treated as an important decorative element in a home. Around the fireplaces, colorful transferware tiles from Britain, Delft tiles from Holland, American Arts and Craft tiles, or other types of tiles added a layer of color to a room and added decoration when the fireplace wasn't being used.

I wanted to add more color and pattern to our cozy library in the form of my own hand-painted tiles. I purchased blank bisqueware tiles and painted them with different colors of underglaze. I painted a mini pattern design so that every tile is different. Unless you have a ceramic kiln like I do, look for a pottery studio that's open to the public and inquire about blank tiles. They will add a gloss glaze to your tiles and fire them.

To install the tiles, my friend Kevin cut a piece of cement board the width of the tiles to fit into the opening inside the wooden mantel. I applied the tiles to the cement board using mastic and grouted them with dark gray grout. The surround is held in place with three pieces of molding that are nailed into the wooden mantel. The entire piece can be easily removed if the next homeowner doesn't like my artwork.

SUPPLIES

Undecorated ceramic bisqueware tiles (mine were 6 inches square)

Pencil and sketchbook

Underglaze for solid color backgrounds (see note)

Black underglaze for painting patterns (see note)

1-inch flat artist's brush for painting tiles

Artist's liner brush in size 10/0 for painting patterns

Newspaper to protect table

Gloss glaze (see note)

FOR THE TILED SURROUND

Cement board cut to fit the fireplace surround

Mastic for applying tiles

Grout for grouting tiles

Putty knife

Trowel for applying mastic

Rubber gloves

Tile cutter

Hot water and bucket

Green scouring pad

Large sponge for wiping grout

½-inch wood molding cut to fit interior of mantel

Paint to match mantel color

Hammer and 1-inch nails

NOTE: If you are using a pottery studio that's open to the public to make this project, you'll likely need to work with the glazes they have. I used a variety of Amaco underglazes for the background colors and black underglaze for the patterns. Request that the studio apply a gloss glaze before firing to make the tiles shiny and easy to clean.

1. Measure the fireplace opening. Have a piece of cement board cut to fit the opening. The opening at my fireplace was 6 inches deep all the way around and 35 inches high by 50 inches wide. Determine how many tiles you will need to cover the opening. I used 18 tiles. I suggest painting some extras in case you have some that don't come out of the kiln perfectly.

2. Cover the table with newspaper. Lay out the tiles. Using different colors of underglaze and the 1-inch brush, paint the tiles in a solid color. Let the underglaze dry and paint 2 more coats. This step will make the background color opaque.

3. Treat each tile uniquely. Using the liner brush, paint a pattern on each tile. To begin, draw some ideas in a sketchbook. Once you begin, the ideas will keep coming. Refer to the pattern illustrations on pages 5 to 10 for ideas. Start at the vertical middle of the tile and work the pattern out to each side. Don't worry about being perfect. The overall effect will be stunning.

4. Have the pottery studio fire your tiles. Ask them to add a gloss glaze so there is a shiny, washable surface.

5. Lay the cement board on a large table. Determine the color placement of the tiles. To do this, figure out how many tiles you will need across the top of the surround. Place a tile at each corner and then fill the remaining space with tiles leaving at least ¼ inch to ½ inch between for grout. Some tiles at the edges may need to be cut to fit properly.

6. Wearing rubber gloves and using a trowel, begin applying mastic at a top corner of the surround. Apply the mastic to the cement board in sections of about 14 inches across the top of the surround. Place the tile in the mastic, lining it up at the outer edge of the cement board. Use a putty knife to tap it into place. Squish it down into the mastic so that it is firmly in place. Lay the next tile ¼ inch to ½ inch away. Continue across the top of the surround, lining up the other corner exactly to the edge of the cement board.

7. Continue laying tiles down the sides of the surround. Cut the bottom tile to fit using a tile cutter. Let the mastic dry overnight.

8. Using grout and wearing rubber gloves, apply the grout between each tile. Using the straight edge of the trowel, wipe off excess grout. Once you are finished, use the sponge soaked in hot water and rub it over each grout line. This step settles the grout into place. Let the grout dry overnight.

9. Using a green scouring pad and hot water, remove the excess grout that has dried.

10. Paint the molding to match the wooden mantelpiece. I used black spray paint.

11. Install the fireplace surround in the opening. Lean it in place. Using the molding, tack it into the wooden mantel with a hammer and nails, taking care not to hit the tiles.

HAND-PAINTED FAUX WALLPAPER

> **PATTERN STYLE:** Geometric
> **PATTERN REPEAT:** Straight
> **TECHNIQUE:** Painting

I have always loved the look of patterned wallpaper. Unfortunately, my tastes are more than my finances allow. When I was thinking about the evolution of our library, I knew I wanted it to be a warm and welcoming space—a room that no one would ever want to leave. I knew that adding a hand-painted pattern to the walls would make the room cozy and comfortable—like one of the libraries that I lust for when I watch BBC historical television series filmed in a manor home in the British countryside.

To get started, I reached for my much-referenced and beat-up paperback copy of Auguste Racinet's *Sourcebook of Historic Ornament*. I found a page with illustrations of Byzantine patterns of Italian marble floors. I did a quick sketch to simplify and tweak the design. Reaching for what was at hand, I cut open some Fedex shipping envelopes, which are made of nice cardstock, and went about drawing some templates using a graph ruler and salad plates as circular guides.

This wallpaper is made by tracing around the templates with a pencil. I painted the shapes by hand using artist's paintbrushes. I used artist's acrylic paints so the shapes would appear slightly transparent and the colors in previous layers would show through slightly. You can also use small tester jars of latex paint available from the paint section of any home store, but these acrylic paints are more opaque.

SUPPLIES

Drop cloth

Latex paint for background (see note)

Poster board

Templates A–D (see page 173)

Scissors

X-Acto knife

Artist's acrylics in assorted colors (see note)

Deli containers with lids for mixing and storing paints

Artist's paintbrushes in assorted sizes

Liner brush in size 1

Water

Rags

NOTE: For the background color, I used a mossy green in a flat latex paint. For the details, I used red, apricot, medium teal, butter yellow, orange, and black artist's acrylics.

1. Spread the drop cloth on the floor. Prep the walls, repairing any holes and dings with spackle.

2. Paint the base color.

3. Enlarge the templates using a copy machine. Cut out the templates. Tape the templates to the poster board. Cut around the templates.

4. Begin at the corner of the room. Fold Template A (cross) in half. Hold it in the upper corner of the room and, using a pencil, trace around it. Continue down the corner of the room butting the motifs together. (See Figure 1.) Next, determine the position of the next template on one of the adjoining walls. Using a builder's level, draw a straight line down the wall at the center point of where the center of the cross motif should be. Use the fold to line up the cross and trace around it. Continue down the wall and then across the wall until the entire space is filled with the cross motif.

5. Using your chosen color (I used red) and an artist's brush, carefully fill in each cross motif with paint. By the time you are finished, the paint will be dry enough to begin the next motif.

6. Using Template B (square with triangle protrusions) center it between the crosses. (See Figure 2.) You will notice that its design has small triangles jutting out from the square. These fit perfectly into the cross design. You should not need to measure. Trace around the motif using a pencil.

7. Using a different color of paint (I used apricot) and a large artist's brush, fill in all the motifs.

8. Place Template C (circle) in the center of the last motif and trace around it with a pencil. Using an artist's brush of a medium size, paint the circles. (See Figure 3, upper right and left.) I alternated colors using butter yellow and medium teal across and up and down the wall.

9. Place Template D (4-pointed star with diamond opening in center) in the center of the circle and trace around it with a pencil. (See Figure 3, lower left.) Using an artist's brush of a medium size, paint the stars using your chosen color. (I used orange.)

10. You are almost done! The last step will take a bit more concentration. Using a liner brush, outline each of the shapes in your chosen color. (See Figure 3, lower right.) I used black. When using a liner brush, the paint needs to be thinner. If necessary, thin it with water. Make sure it is not too liquid as to run down the wall. As you are painting, try to vary the pressure of the liner brush to give a wavy effect to the outlines. This technique will give a handmade quality to your faux wallpaper.

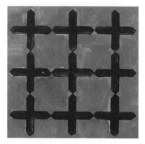

Figure 1

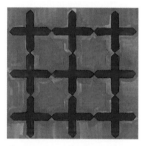

Figure 2

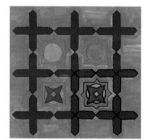

Figure 3

FLOWERS IN VASES DECORATIVE MURAL

PATTERN STYLE: Geometric and Organic
PATTERN REPEAT: Straight
TECHNIQUE: Painting

Between the two south-facing windows in the library, there is a small space about a yard wide—just the perfect size for a small mural. Inspired by memories of the tiles I saw in Portugal at every turn, I designed a scene with "tiles" that would be painted diagonally on the wall. In front of my tiles, I drew two turquoise vases of stylized flowers, reminiscent of the potted plants that thrive in the temperate weather in Portugal.

For this mural, I chose to continue to use the same colors as I did in the Hand-Painted Faux Wallpaper project (see page 89). Once again, I used poster board templates to trace the shapes. For the vases, I free-handed a classic shape. Once the tiles and vases were painted, I free-handed the stems, flowers, and leaves. To finish it all up and add a cohesive feeling to the room, I outlined the images in the mural with black paint and a liner brush, just like I did for the motifs in the faux wallpaper.

SUPPLIES

Drop cloth

Scissors

X-Acto knife

Latex paint for background (see note)

Poster board

Templates A–F (see pages 174–75)

Artist's acrylics in assorted colors (see note)

Deli containers with lids for mixing paints

Artist's paintbrushes in assorted sizes

Liner brush in size 1

Water

Rags for cleanup

NOTE: For the background color I used a mossy green in a flat latex paint. For the details, I used red, apricot, teal, butter yellow, orange, dark teal, and black.

1. Spread the drop cloth on the floor. Prep the walls, repairing any holes and dings with spackle.

2. Paint the base color.

3. Enlarge the templates using a copy machine. Cut out the templates. Tape the templates to the poster board. Cut around the templates using scissors or an X-Acto knife.

4. Begin with the Template A (vase). Place it where you want it and trace around it with a pencil. Repeat for the second vase.

5. Determine the center of the space. Using a builder's level and pencil and beginning at the ceiling, draw a vertical line down the wall. This line will act as a guide for placing the faux tiles. Place Template B (large diamond) with the points lined up along the vertical line and trace it. Continue down the wall, covering the vertical line with diamonds.

6. Repeat Step 5, moving to the right and left of the center row of diamonds. When you reach your vase outlines, continue to trace around the diamonds but leave the vases empty.

7. Paint the diamonds. (I alternated vertical rows of red and butter yellow.) Make sure to leave the vase spaces empty.

8. Using Template C (large circle), eyeball the placement in the center of each diamond and trace. The circle motif is placed every other row (I placed mine on the butter yellow diamonds).

9. Paint the circles. Using an artist's paintbrush and your chosen color, fill in the circles. (I used orange.)

10. Using Template D (small diamond), eyeball the placement in the center of each diamond and trace it. The diamond motif is placed every other row in the empty diamonds.

11. Paint the smaller diamonds. Using an artist's paintbrush and your chosen color, fill in the diamonds. (I used teal.)

12. Using Template E (small circle), eyeball the placement in the center of each circle and trace it. The smaller circle motif is placed in each circle.

13. Paint the circles. Using an artist's paintbrush and your chosen color, fill in the circles. (I used mossy green.)

14. Using Template F (4-pointed star), eyeball the placement in the center of each diamond and trace it. The star motif is placed every other row in the diamond motifs.

15. Paint the stars. Using an artist's paintbrush and your chosen color, fill in the stars. (I used apricot.)

16. Paint the vases. (I used dark teal.)

17. Using a pencil, freehand the outlines of the leaves and flowers on the wall. Do not feel like you have to follow my design exactly. This is your place to put your own spin on the mural.

18. Using various colors, paint the flowers, stems, and leaves.

19. Using a dark color (I used black) and the liner brush, outline all the shapes. When using a liner brush, the paint needs to be thinner. If necessary, thin with water. Make sure it is not too liquid as to run down the wall. As you are painting, try to vary the pressure of the liner brush to give a wavy effect to the outlines. This variety in the line will give a handmade quality to your faux wallpaper.

CHAPTER THREE

BATHROOM
AND
BEDROOM

UPSTAIRS IS WHERE WE GO TO REST AND REPLENISH OURSELVES FOR THE NEXT DAY. FOR THE PRIVATE SPACES IN OUR HOME, I WANTED TO INVOKE A FEELING OF CALM—A REMINDER OF SUMMER CHILDHOOD DAYS, TAKING AN AFTERNOON NAP WITH THE WINDOWS OPEN AND WASH DRYING ON THE line when there was not a care in my world. Flowers, antique floral prints, and hand-embroidered linens were the inspiration for these quieter rooms that we use as we wind down from our busy lives.

The bathroom is light and bright and cheerful. British transferware tiles from the Victorian era, collected over the years, inspired the decoration of the bathroom. Covered with delicate, pretty flowers, these tiles look lovely against the hand-painted wallpaper. A claw-foot tub decorated with a design derivative of airy hand-stitched embroidery is the perfect place for a soak and to relax. The ecru-colored wood wainscoting gives a feeling of bygone days and peace and quiet.

The bedroom is decorated in gold and green colors that in the winter give a reminder of warmer days. For many years, we grew a field of sunflowers, and they have become a theme of our family life here on our farm. Three walls of the bedroom are covered with hand-painted sunflower blossoms that create a cheerful feeling in the room. Wooden furniture collected over the years came together in an unplanned way and creates an old-fashioned feeling of comfort and stability—so key to the start of each day before chaos sets in. Bits of blue, magenta, sage green, and turquoise on the floor, bed, lampshades, and artwork give pops of color that add to the pleasant feeling of the room. Pattern isn't everywhere, and it's used in a more restrained manner than in the public areas of the farmhouse.

COMBED STOOL

> **PATTERN STYLE:** Organic
> **PATTERN REPEAT:** Random
> **TECHNIQUE:** Painting

Every bathroom needs a step stool for small people. I purchased this stool at an unfinished-furniture store for my daughter Julia to stand on when she wasn't big enough to see in the mirror. To dress it up a little, I did a fun paint technique called "combing." This type of paint treatment has been around for hundreds of years. It is very simple and easy to do, and you probably have all the supplies in your home right now.

I used a homemade combing tool that I cut out of a cereal box. You could also use an old gift box or credit card. Plastic comb tools can be purchased from specialty faux finish suppliers, but they really aren't necessary. This paint treatment can also be done on walls, doors, and furniture. Choose two paint colors that have high contrast so the design can be seen easily.

Small piece of furniture

Latex paint in 2 colors
(1 dark and 1 light)

Paintbrush

Cereal box

Template (see page 176)

Scissors or X-Acto knife

Polyurethane

1. Wash and prepare the furniture for painting.

2. Paint the entire piece with a color that will be revealed when combing. I used blue.

3. The next steps need to be done in various stages so the piece can dry properly. Begin with the top. Paint a thick layer of your second color of paint over the first color. Immediately, pull the comb through the paint to create a design so the bottom color shows through. You can make straight lines, diagonal lines, or squiggly lines. My stool features wavy lines. You must use wet fresh paint in order to remove the color and make the designs. Let this section dry.

4. Continue in this manner—allowing the previous section to dry then starting with fresh, wet paint on another section—until you have done all the spaces on the piece that you want decorated.

5. Protect with 2 to 3 coats of polyurethane.

BATHROOM FAUX WALLPAPER

> PATTERN STYLE: Geometric
> PATTERN REPEAT: Straight
> TECHNIQUE: Painting

The wainscoting on the walls is the primary feature of the bathroom. Above it, there is a small space that was free for a paint or paper treatment. I decided to paint very wide, vertical stripes using painter's tape as my guide. Wide, painted stripes add a festive and bold look to any space. The walls were already colorwashed in a pretty gold color. Using painter's tape, I measured 8½-inch sections, because that was the width of my gridded ruler. (Sometimes I just go with what is easy!) I painted a washy/streaky coat of white paint. It called for even more decoration.

I folded some paper that was the length of my wall in half vertically and horizontally cut an S curve along the open edge to create an ogee design. I decided on a pretty blue color to fill the space. The resulting "wallpaper" is bold and elegant at the same time. The Victorian tiles and prints that I have hung on the walls look like they really belong with the new wall treatment.

SUPPLIES

18 × 24-inch drawing paper or poster board (see note)	Painter's tape
Scissors	Latex paint in 2 colors (see note)
Builder's level	1-inch paintbrush (see note)
Graph ruler	Ladder
Pencil	Drop cloth

NOTE: I used latex paint in white and blue. For the paintbrush, I used a 1-inch chip brush to create the streaky quality. If you want to try out the design before putting paint to the wall, use a large piece of paper and paint the actual design you are thinking of. Hang it on the wall and live with it for a few days to see if you like it. Then go ahead and paint your walls. If your wall is longer than the ogee template, trace a second ogee on top of the first to create a longer shape. This design would look excellent covering an entire wall or room.

1. Determine the height and width of your ogee shape. Cut a piece of paper the length and width needed. Fold it in half vertically and then horizontally. Cut the paper on the open (non-folded) edge in a curve. Open the paper to see if you like the shape. Refold and adjust until you're happy with it. This design is very versatile and can be made thinner, wider, longer, or shorter depending on the space and scale that your room offers. Tape the template to the drawing paper or poster board and cut out the shape.

2. Paint the stripes. Using a builder's level, draw vertical pencil lines on the wall. Apply painter's tape along the vertical lines. My stripes are 8½ inches wide. Press firmly so that the paint will not seep under the tape.

3. Roughly brush paint between the taped lines to create wide stripes. (I used white.) Let the paint dry. Remove the tape.

4. Paint the S curve. Place the ogee tape in the middle of the white stripes and trace with a faint pencil line. Using your chosen paint color, roughly brush the paint between the pencil lines. (I used blue.) I recommend painting the edges first and then filling in the large shape between the S curves.

STRIPED LAMPSHADE

> **PATTERN STYLE:** Geometric
> **PATTERN REPEAT:** Straight
> **TECHNIQUE:** Painting

I have made a large assortment of hand-painted lampshades that are used throughout our home. When lit at night, they cast a colorful glow throughout the living spaces. From the outside looking in, they resemble stained glass. For the Sunflower Bedroom, I knew that I would need a graphic lampshade design so that the shade would stand out against the wildly patterned wall design. I decided upon wide stripes in the complementary colors lupine blue and bright yellow. As I was painting it, I couldn't help but think of wide-striped awnings providing shade at the seashore. This is a rather simple design to paint and a perfect choice if you are a beginner.

SUPPLIES

White fabric lampshade, preferably cotton with styrene backing

Drop cloth

Jacquard Textile Color fabric paint in various colors (see note)

Jacquard Textile Color #100 Colorless Extender (see note)

Versatex Fixative

Small deli or yogurt containers

Auto-fade or vanishing fabric marker

Artist's paintbrush in large flat size

Water

Muslin fabric scraps for practicing painting and testing colors

NOTE: For my lampshades, I used sapphire blue, neon pink, goldenrod, and yellow. I use more Colorless Extender than paint color when painting lampshades. The extender makes the colors more translucent so that the light will shine through. To experiment, paint some samples and let the paint dry. Hang them in front of a lamp in the evening to see the effect you will get. Do not add white to lighten the paint colors as it will make the lampshade more opaque. Do not add water to the textile paint as it will make it run on the lampshade and produce blurred designs.

1. Spread the drop cloth on your working surface. Mix your colors to your liking. To produce the lupine blue color, I mixed a small bit of neon pink with sapphire blue. For my yellow, I mixed the goldenrod and yellow together. Thin your textile colors with Colorless Extender to get the desired translucency (see note). Add Versatex Fixer following the manufacturer's directions.

2. Practice painting stripes on the muslin fabric to get the feel for the paint on fabric. It will actually be easier on the shade because the fabric is stretched tightly.

3. Begin painting your lampshade. Use an auto-fade fabric marker or very light pencil lines to lay out the stripes if desired. I freehand my stripes so that they have a bit of a hand-painted, wobbly look.

4. Paint the stripes in the darker color, spacing them equally around the shade.

5. Fill in the empty spaces with the lighter color. If the colors overlap, it will create a third color. Let the paint dry.

DOTS AND SPOTS PILLOW

⬡
PATTERN STYLE: Geometric
PATTERN REPEAT: Brick
TECHNIQUE: Stamping and Stitching
⬡

When I was a little girl, I used to stay overnight at my grandmother's house and sleep in the bed that was my dad's when he was a little boy. On the bed, there was a handmade quilt. The pillowcases were embroidered by my grandmother with flowers and leaves in colorful cotton embroidery thread. I remember being fascinated with all the handwork I was sleeping among and thinking to myself that I would like to learn to make things like that one day. As I got older, Gram taught me to embroider. Soon the lingo of the craft—chain stitch, French knots, outline stitch, and more—became familiar to me in language and in actual stitching. That early introduction to hand-stitched things for the home has become the central passion of my life.

The Dots and Spots Pillow is a fun and easy project to make. Begin by printing giant dots on some linen. Then add miniature "spots" around each giant dot by stitching French knots. I love the graphic look of this pillow and think it adds a modern touch to the bedroom. The techniques of hand printing and hand embroidery make an interesting dichotomy to think about. This pillow plays the handmade domestic arts against a modern, hard-edged graphic pillow design.

SUPPLIES

FOR THE STAMP

Template (see page 176)

Craft foam with adhesive backing for making stamp

1-inch-thick foam building insulation

Scissors

Tape

Utility knife

FOR THE PILLOW

⅝ yard of linen fabric in green

⅝ yard of colorful backing fabric

Steam iron

Drop cloth

Jacquard Textile Color in navy blue

Versatex Fixer, optional

1-inch foam brush

Deli container with lid

Table for printing

Fabric and craft scissors

Crewel wool embroidery thread in hot pink, red, and fuchsia

Chenille needle

Sewing machine

24 × 16-inch down pillow insert

FINISHED SIZE: 24 × 16 inches

1. Prewash the linen and the backing fabric and hang it to dry. Iron it with a steam iron to smooth out the wrinkles. Cut the linen fabric to measure 25 × 17 inches. Follow the directions for cutting the backing fabric (see "Basic Technique: Making an Easy Throw Pillow" on page 38).

2. Using the template and following the instructions, assemble the foam stamp (see "Basic Techniques: Making Stamps" on page 33).

3. Cover a table with a canvas drop cloth to become a printing surface.

4. Fold the linen rectangle in half both width-wise and lengthwise, matching raw edges. Press along the fold to create guidelines.

5. Follow the instructions for printing with foam stamps (see "Stamping Tips" on page 32). Begin at the center point of the pillow and use the folds for placing the center circle at the center of the fabric. Print 2 circles on each side of the center circle, placing them 2½ inches apart centered along the horizontal fold—5 circles total.

6. Print 4 circles, placing the bottom of the circle ¼ inch down from the top of the first row of circles in the middle line. This is called a brick pattern. Repeat to create a third row below the center row of circles. Print 1 more row of circles above and below the last rows of circles. The new row should match up with the center row of circles vertically and be placed ¼ inch in from the circle row above or below.

7. Embroidery: Using a double strand of crewel wool, work French knots evenly around the circles, approximately ¼ inch away from the edge and spaced about ¼ inch apart. (See "French Knot" on page 80 for instructions.) Alternate colors around each circle.

8. Sew the pillow (see "Basic Technique: Making an Easy Throw Pillow" on page 38).

AMISH-INSPIRED DUVET COVER

PATTERN STYLE: Geometric
PATTERN REPEAT: Straight
TECHNIQUE: Stitching

I have always found the quilts that the Amish people make extremely beautiful. Considering that the Amish wear such somber clothing, they really pull out the colorful stops when sewing quilts. Many of their quilt designs feature simple geometric patterns that are easy to piece and sew. This Amish-inspired duvet cover is a nice project for beginning piecers.

We use down comforters and wool blankets in our home to keep the cold away. Instead of making a traditional quilt, I turned the pieced top layer into a duvet cover. You could quilt it if you like. I chose colors that would contrast with the Sunflower Faux Wallpaper and make a graphic statement on the bed. The simple design is a great way to play with colors, and it could be easily modified to fit a crib or different bed size.

For the backing, I designed my own fabric. Beginning with a lino-cut sunflower motif, I colored it different ways in Adobe Illustrator and had the fabric printed at Spoonflower.

Selecting the colors and fabrics for your duvet cover is where the fun starts. Use the template provided to design your own color version. To do this, photocopy the chart onto cardstock. Cut small pieces of fabric in colors or prints of your own choosing. Attach the colors to the chart with double-sided tape. You can play all you want with them until you have a design you like. Use the chart as your road map when sewing the quilt.

SUPPLIES

13½ yards of 45-inch quilting cotton as follows (see note):

- ½ yard each in colors coral and gold
- 1¾ yards each in lapis blue and pickle
- 1¼ yards in pomegranate
- 2½ yards in cinnamon for the border

5¼ yards of 45-inch cotton quilting fabric or more for the backing (see note)

Steam iron

Graph ruler

Sewing machine and sewing thread

Rotary fabric cutter

Scissors

Seam ripper

One 54-inch zipper (available from upholstery stores) or hook-and-loop fastener

FINISHED SIZE: 90 × 90 inches to fit a queen size down comforter. To adjust size, increase or decrease the border pieces in length and width.

NOTE: For this duvet, I used Kona cotton fabric, which is easy to find at quilting shops and comes in hundreds of colors. For the backing, note that if you use a print that needs to be matched, you may need more fabric than specified.

Use a ½-inch seam allowance when sewing all pieces.

1. Wash the fabrics to preshrink, and dry in a dryer. Remove before completely dry and iron them with a steam iron to smooth out any wrinkles.

2. Using a rotary cutter, cut your fabrics as follows:

   · CENTER: Cut 3 pieces, 9 × 41 inches, in lapis; for pieced square stripes, cut 20 pieces, each 5 × 5 inches, in both coral and gold.

   · INSIDE BORDER: Cut 4 pieces, 9 × 41 inches, in pomegranate; 4 pieces, 9 × 9 inches, in lapis.

   · MIDDLE BORDER: Cut 8 pieces, 9 × 29 inches, in pickle; 4 pieces, 9 × 9 inches, in lapis.

   · OUTSIDE BORDER: Cut 4 pieces, 10 × 46 inches, and 4 pieces, 10 × 37 inches, in cinnamon.

3. Following the chart, sew the center 5 × 5 squares together, alternating between colors, to make the center check sections. Make 2 strips of squares with a total of 20 squares each.

4. Sew the check strips to the solid lapis color strips following the chart.

5. Sew the inside border. Sew 1 strip of pomegranate to the top and bottom of the center panel. Sew 1 lapis block at each end of the remaining 2 pomegranate strips. Sew these strips to the center section, matching the seams.

6. Sew the middle border. Sew two 9 × 29-inch pickle pieces together along the short side to make a long strip of fabric 9 × 57 inches long. Repeat 3 more times with the remaining pieces. Sew 1 strip at both the top and bottom of the middle section. Sew 1 lapis block at each end of the remaining 2 pickle strips. Sew these strips to the center section, matching the seams.

7. Sew the outer border. Sew two 37 × 10-inch border strips together on 1 short side to make the top border. Repeat for the bottom border. Sew two 46 × 10-inch strips together on 1 short side to make 1 side border. Repeat for the opposite side.

8. Sew the 2 short borders to the top and bottom of the quilt. Sew the longer borders to each side of the quilt.

9. Piece the backing. Cut 2 pieces of the back cover fabric 91 inches long. Sew them together along 1 selvage edge. Measure your patchwork top and adjust the width of the back fabric to match the width of the top, making sure the seam on the back fabric remains in the center.

10. Place the pieced top and the back fabric with the right sides together, aligning all edges. At the bottom edge, determine the center of the piece and mark it. Pin the bottom edge. Center the zipper and mark the 2 endpoints of the zipper opening with pins or a marker. (See Figure 1.) Sew along the bottom edge, beginning with a regular-length stitch, changing to a basting-length stitch when you reach the mark where the zipper will begin,

then changing back to a regular-length stitch for the remainder of the seam after you pass the other mark showing the end of the zipper. Press the seam open.

11. Inset the zipper using the centering method. (See Figure 2.) Place the right side of the zipper toward the basted seam, centering it. Pin it in place. Using a zipper foot, stitch across the bottom of the zipper, stitch ⅜ inch away from the zipper up 1 side, stitch across the other end of the zipper, then stitch down the remaining side ⅜ inch away from the zipper. After the zipper is sewn in, remove the basting stitches with a seam ripper.

12. With right sides together and the zipper partly open, pin and sew the remaining 3 sides of the duvet cover to the backing as if you were making a giant pillow. Clip the corners diagonally. Turn the cover right side out. Press and insert your duvet.

Figure 1

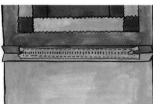

Figure2

SUNFLOWER FAUX WALLPAPER

PATTERN STYLE: Organic
PATTERN REPEAT: Random
TECHNIQUE: Painting

It is cold and dark here in New England for six months of every year. Although we get accustomed to the shorter days, we always pine for the longer daylight hours of summer. To bring a little summer all year long into our bedroom, I painted giant sunflower blossoms over three walls. The room is now joyful and sunny every day of the year.

I began by painting three of the walls a warm golden ochre color. The east-facing wall—where the sun rises—was painted a rich green shade to echo the leaves that are on the ancient maple tree outside the window. Inspiration for the sunflower "wallpaper" came from the field of sunflowers Mark and I grew for many years along on a busy road in the next town over. We grow hay now, not sunflowers, but the field is still called "The Sunflower Field." Old habits die hard in New England.

If you don't want to paint an entire room with sunflowers, try the faux wallpaper technique on only one wall in a room or in a small space, perhaps between windows. It would also be great in a bathroom.

SUPPLIES

18 × 24-inch drawing paper or poster board

Templates (see pages 178–79)

Scissors

Pencil

Painter's tape

Latex paint (see note)

Artist's paintbrushes in various sizes

Ladder

Drop cloth

NOTE: For this project, use latex paint in a flat or satin finish. I used yellow, gold, green, and brown. My sunflowers are 4 different sizes but you could choose only 1 or 2 of the templates. All the leaves are drawn freehand, which gives you the chance to vary the number and size of the leaves that surround each flower. Practice on a piece of paper if you are fearful of drawing a leaf yourself. Two curved lines with a point make a leaf.

1. Enlarge the templates to the desired size and cut out. Tape them to the drawing paper or poster board and cut out the shapes.

2. Position the templates where you want them and tape to the wall. Trace around the shapes with a pencil. Vary the spacing and the sizes as you place them around the room. Remember to leave space for the leaves.

3. Cover the floor with the drop cloth. Using the flower color, fill in the shapes with the paint (I used light yellow). I put my paint on a bit thin so that it would look washy and give a bit of texture to the flowers.

4. Using the center flower color (I used gold), paint the center using loose circular strokes. Again, allow the color below to show through a bit.

5. For the leaves, draw them freehand, referring to my photo. Draw 1, 2, or 3 leaves around each flower. Fill them in with the paint color desired (I used green).

6. Using a dark color and a round paintbrush, paint the outlines for the petals, flower center, leaves, and center veins (I used dark brown).

DIAMOND MOTIF CLOSETS

> **PATTERN STYLE:** Geometric
> **PATTERN REPEAT:** Straight
> **TECHNIQUE:** Painting

The Sunflower Bedroom has a large wall of shiplap closets with vertical stripes formed by the pine boards. Instead of painting sunflowers on them, I wanted a more graphic design to contrast with the sunflower motif. It had to be large and bold to match the large scale of the sunflowers. I decided upon a diamond motif. I did a paint technique called "pouncing" to create the mottled surface texture. This project would work nicely on traditional paneled doors too.

SUPPLIES

Acrylic or latex paint

18 × 24-inch drawing paper

Yardstick

Painter's tape

Pencil

1-inch foam dauber for pouncing

Latex paint in desired color

Figure 1

1. Measure the height and width of your closet. Divide the height by 3 to give the height of the diamond. Cut a rectangle the width of the closet by ⅓ of the height. Fold it in 2 lengthwise, then in 2 widthwise, matching the open edges. Draw a diagonal line from the outer tip of the height to the outer tip of the width. Cut along this line. (See Figure 1.) You will have a large diamond.

2. Using small pieces of painter's tape, tape the top diamond at the top center of the closet. Using a pencil, draw along the diamond to create a guide. Repeat 2 more times below the top diamond.

3. Place a line of painter's tape along the pencil line. Tape 1 diamond at a time. Using the dauber, make quick up and down motions, pouncing along the tape to create a mottled diamond. Do not create a solid shape—let the color below show through a bit. You will have 1 straight edge (the edge covered with paint); the inner edge will be bumpy and uneven. Remove the painter's tape immediately so that you can clean up any places where the paint may have seeped under the tape. Let the paint dry.

4. Repeat for each diamond. It is best to paint the diamonds over several hours or days so that the pounced paint color has adequate time to dry.

PART TWO

OUTDOOR SPACES

CHAPTER FOUR

POTTERY STUDIO AND GARDEN SHED

THE HEIRLOOM TOMATO Amy Goldman

APPLE LOVER'S COOKBOOK

I HAVE A LOT OF HOBBIES AND SKILLS THAT I HAVE LEARNED OVER THE YEARS. EACH NEW SKILL BEGETS TOOLS AND SUPPLIES THAT ALL NEED TO BE TAKEN CARE OF SO THEY WILL BE THERE WHEN I NEED THEM AGAIN. WITH THE SEASONS, ACTIVITIES EBB AND FLOW AND I LOOK FORWARD TO FOLLOWING MY YEAR'S PROGRESSION OF MAKING AND doing. As I have grown older, I realize that each of the skills I know, and continue to learn, informs the others. Learning pottery helped me to better understand the sculptural qualities of objects. My love of gardening and flowers led to my colorful painted ceramics decorated with flowers. My love of textiles and pattern has invaded every corner of my creative life.

All these skills and interests and the supplies that they use cross-pollinate and can become a jumbled mess. A place to find focus and inspire creativity for my ceramics and a place to store the tools for gardening were sorely needed. Two under-utilized outdoor sheds had accumulated lots of the debris of life. It was time to conquer the clutter. The smaller building is now a garden shed with walls covered in giant leaves and vines and a brightly colored, rose blossom faux rug. The larger shed is now a pottery studio. Purposely decorated with minimalistic pattern, this space will inspire creativity. Both little sheds are now havens for my creative activities that fuel my life and help me remain inspired to continue to create and do.

PATTERNED PENDANT LAMP

> **PATTERN STYLE:** Organic
> **PATTERN REPEAT:** Random
> **TECHNIQUE:** Painting

The shed has only one overhead outlet for a lamp, which means I had one shot to do something special for the lighting. I wanted something fun and creative looking but also utilitarian and inexpensive. I worked in a textile factory for many years and I was always fond of the metal pendant lamps that were used over the different work benches. I found a similar style for a very reasonable price at the local home supply store. It was a boring silver metal color. To give it the creative vibe I was looking for, I painted it with spray paint and further decorated it with hand-painted motifs. This was a very easy and quick project to do, and it adds a bit of quirkiness to my space.

SUPPLIES

Overhead metal pendant lamp

Drop cloth

Spray paint for the base

Latex paint for decoration

Round artist's paintbrush

1. Work outside or in a well-ventilated area. Cover your work surface with the drop cloth.

2. Follow the manufacturer's directions for the spray paint. Spray the lamp using short bursts of paint. Let it dry. If needed, apply a second coat.

3. Using an artist's brush, paint the lamp. I painted my lamp with squiggly and diagonal lines and half circles and filled in the empty spaces with different-sized dots.

4. Install the lamp.

BLOCK-PRINTED JUG CURTAINS

> **PATTERN STYLE:** Organic
> **PATTERN REPEAT:** Straight
> **TECHNIQUE:** Block Printing

Block printing is simple to do and doesn't require too many expensive supplies. With rubber blocks, some simple carving tools, and a bit of ink, graphic designs are only a step away. The first time you carve a block, it may be a bit confusing. The rubber that is carved away will not print. Any rubber that is left is what will form the image.

When I am carving blocks, I carve in steps. I carve away the key areas of my image and make a sample print. By looking at the print, I can see what other areas I want to take away. When working on this jug block, I carved the jug and printed it. I continued to carve and test until I was happy with the motif.

Although carving blocks isn't the most intuitive skill, with a little practice your brain will begin to adapt to how each motif is created. Blocks can be used to print fabric, as I did here, and paper too. Wash the ink off the blocks so you can use them over and over again.

SUPPLIES

White cotton curtains

3 × 4-inch Speedwell Speedy-Carve block

Linoleum carving tools (see "Cutting and Carving Tools" on page 39)

Template (see page 177)

Pencil

Speedball Fabric Block Printing Ink in blue

Sheet of Plexiglas for spreading ink

Brayer

Drop cloth

Printing surface

Muslin fabric for practice printing

1. Wash and dry the curtains. Iron them to remove any wrinkles.

2. Photocopy the jug template or design your own.

3. On the back of the template, rub a pencil so that the back is covered with graphite. Turn the template over and place it centered on top of the block with the graphite side facing the block. With a pen or pencil, trace the outlines of the motif. The graphite should transfer to the block.

4. Using the linoleum cutting tools, carve around the lines. Remember: Uncarved areas will print; carved areas will not print. Carving tools come in different widths and shapes. Use the larger ones to carve away the background. Use the smaller tips for the details.

5. Spread your drop cloth on a table. Spread the curtain out on the surface to ready it for printing.

6. Squeeze some ink onto the piece of Plexiglas. If you want to mix a special color, do it now with a palette knife.

7. Roll the brayer through the ink to spread it. Using the brayer, roll the ink onto the block.

8. With the ink side down, press the block onto the muslin to practice printing. Once you feel comfortable, print the motif as desired onto the curtain. I made a row of jugs along the bottom of the curtain. For spacing, make a small guide from a piece of paper to keep the motifs evenly spaced.

WALL WITH STAMPED BORDER

> **PATTERN STYLE:** Geometric
> **PATTERN REPEAT:** Straight
> **TECHNIQUE:** Stamping

SUPPLIES

Builder's level

Pencil

Painter's tape

Latex paint in semi-gloss
and various colors

Paintbrushes, rollers,
and tray

Drop cloth

Household sponges

Scissors

Marker for drawing
on sponges

Although I am a huge fan of lots of color in my home, in my art studios I prefer having lots of white space. My painting, textile designs, and ceramics are very colorful. White walls give me a bright, clean backdrop to hang colorful inspiration photos. That said, for the pottery studio, I needed some fun color to draw me in to the creative space.

I decided upon a color-block design for the walls that would echo the floor design. I painted the top half of the walls and ceiling off-white and applied different colors below the windows—periwinkle blue, lime green, turquoise, and lupine blue. The studio is bright and cheerful and a perfect backdrop for creating my colorful pottery. To add to the creative vibe I was going for, I stamped a border above each color using household sponges that I cut into geometric shapes.

1. Using a builder's level and pencil, draw a horizontal line at the bottom of each window across the wall.

2. Run a line of painter's tape above the line to create a border.

3. Protect the floor with the drop cloth. Paint the lower half of each wall with your chosen color using brushes and a roller. Let the paint dry. Apply a second coat. Let it dry and remove the tape.

4. Cut the sponges into desired shapes. I used 2 different triangles and a half circle for stamping. Draw your shape onto the sponge and cut it out with scissors.

5. Pour a small amount of paint into a paint tray. Dip 1 side of the dry sponge into the paint and stamp the wall. Do not use a wet sponge or the paint may drip. Try to keep the sponge a bit dry so it will create an interesting texture. Continue stamping the shapes along each horizontal border and around the windows. Each dip of the sponge into the paint tray will yield several stamps. Let the paint dry.

COLOR-BLOCKED FLOOR

┌─────────────────────────────────┐
PATTERN STYLE: Geometric
PATTERN REPEAT: Random
TECHNIQUE: Tiling
└─────────────────────────────────┘

The pottery studio's floor was raw plywood. Because working with clay is so messy, I wanted a floor surface that would be easy to clean. Stashed in our basement were some vinyl composition tiles (VCT) leftover from another project. VCT tile is used in schools, hospitals, grocery stores—places where it goes unnoticed. It is incredibly durable and easy to clean, and what most people don't know, is that it is available in over 400 colors. I had nine colors of brightly colored tile—but not equal amounts of each. I made a list of the number of each tile color I had available and set to work on designing a colorful floor.

This project was similar to designing a patchwork quilt—I was assembling blocks of color into different patterns. I designed two floors. The first was a diamond quilt design and the second was a color-blocked modern-looking Mondrian-inspired version. I let the ideas sit for a couple days as I weighed the pros and cons of both designs. I find that if I have time, it helps to have an interior design simmer in my brain while I think it through.

I decided upon the modern design because I thought it would be a perfect colorful backdrop for my work. With the studio supplies, potter's wheel, and furniture that I knew would be scattered across the floor, I felt the diamond quilt design would be lost. My friends and I installed the floor in less than a day.

SUPPLIES

Assorted colors of vinyl composition tile (mine was made by Armstrong Flooring)

Vinyl tile glue adhesive

Trowel for spreading adhesive

VCT tile cutter (available for rent) or chop saw

Putty knife or scraper for removing excess glue

Hot water and bucket

Green scouring pad for removing dried glue

1. Measure the floor. Using graph paper, draw the floor space to scale. Decide upon the colors of tile and determine the amount needed to cover the square foot area. Using colored pencils, markers, or a computer program, draw several design ideas for your floor. Choose the design you like best as your design map and purchase the amount of tile needed. Determine the exact center of the room and mark it on the drawing.

2. Pick a nice, warm, dry day to install the tile. The glue needs a full 24 to 48 hours to set up before you can walk on it. Determine the exact center of the room. Begin at the center of the room, working toward the 4 corners. Work in sections, remembering that you need to get out of the room once the floor is down.

3. Spread the adhesive following the manufacturer's instructions. Avoid making the adhesive too thick, as it will ooze to the top of the tile and be difficult to clean up. Place the tiles, butting them right next to each other. Follow the design map that you have drawn.

4. Continue working. When you get to the corners, cut the tiles to fit the space.

5. Let the adhesive dry without walking on it, following the manufacturer's recommendations.

6. Once the adhesive is dry, remove any excess with a putty knife. Wash the floor. Using the green scouring pad, remove any excess adhesive. Seal the tile if desired with VCT tile sealer.

MAUD LEWIS

Maud Lewis was a Canadian folk artist born in Nova Scotia in 1903. She suffered from juvenile rheumatoid arthritis that disfigured her body and caused her great pain. Her mother taught her how to paint with watercolors and she began her art career selling the watercolors for Christmas cards. Her style was very naïve and colorful. Maud's parents died when she was a young adult and she went to live with an aunt. Her artwork became her occupation as she was disabled and unable to hold a normal job.

Maud married Everett Lewis after answering his advertisement for a live-in housekeeper. Together they lived in his very small one-room house without any electricity or modern plumbing. Encouraged by Everett, Maud continued to paint her cards. Eventually she painted naïve-style paintings on cookie sheets and Masonite boards using discarded oil paints that Everett procured from boat

owners at the nearby fishing village. She began selling her paintings outside of their home for a couple dollars apiece. She painted country scenes of horses, carriages, oxen, cats, birds, boats, and the ocean. Her artwork was colorful and simple and very happy feeling.

Maud painted their very small home both inside and out with her signature folk-style designs of flowers, butterflies, birds, trees, cats, vases, and more. Every surface of the home was covered with colorful images, including the stove, the breadbox, and stairway. On the exterior, flowers and butterflies, birds and trees decorated the shingled building. After Maud and Everett died, the home was rescued from disintegration by concerned citizens who did not want the building to disappear. It was fully restored and is now installed at the Art Gallery of Nova Scotia. Maud's paintings are now in collections all over the world.

EXTERIOR WINDOW MURALS

PATTERN STYLE: Organic
PATTERN REPEAT: Straight
TECHNIQUE: Painting

When renovating spaces, decorating opportunities sometimes arise that are not planned. When my old kitchen window needed to be replaced, I had it installed in the pottery shed. It replaced a longer row of non-functioning windows. The construction left raw plywood on either side of the newly placed window. Instead of trying to match the stain that had been aging on the shed for years, I decided to do something decorative.

I have been inspired by the painted folk-style floral paintings of Canadian artist Maud Lewis (see page 131). I channeled my inner Maud and painted two different patterned vases filled with flowers on both sides of the newly placed window. My design was painted entirely freehand. I worked on each side quickly and without much planning. I find that if I work in the moment and don't worry too much, I end up with a more spontaneous end product. The rough surface of the plywood allowed an interesting textural quality to develop in the paintings. For patterns, I decorated the jugs with polka dots and squiggly lines.

SUPPLIES

Primer to prep the area

Tester jars of latex paint in your favorite colors

Various artist's brushes

Ladder

Water for cleanup

Polyurethane for weather protection

1. Wash the area and let it dry.

2. Prime the space where the mural is going. Let the paint dry.

3. Pencil in the vases and some circles to represent the flower centers.

4. Paint the flowers.

5. Add some leaves and stems. Make some hang down over the vase to make the illustration look more natural.

6. Paint the vase in a solid color. Decorate the vase with stripes and polka dots.

7. Paint the background around the flowers and vases. I let the white primer show through a bit to make an interesting texture.

8. Step back and see how it looks. If you have time, wait a day to review the mural; then, add more bits if needed.

9. Using a liner brush, paint the outlines of the vases, flowers, and leaves to give more definition to the mural.

10. Because this is an exterior mural, apply 2 to 3 coats of polyurethane to protect it from rain and sun exposure.

JACK AND THE BEANSTALK FAUX WALLPAPER

> PATTERN STYLE: Organic
> PATTERN REPEAT: Random
> TECHNIQUE: Painting

The garden shed was the former playhouse for our daughter, Julia, who is now nineteen. It was the perfect size to become a garden shed and to bring order to all my gardening tools. I wanted the shed to have a fantasy feeling to it—a place where I could sit down, make plant lists, order seeds, and dream about the garden that could be. After all, growing a garden is a lot about dreams of what is to come and the faith to plant, tend, and wait for the beauty and bounty.

When decorating the walls of the shed, I remembered the child's fairy tale *Jack and the Beanstalk*. I decided to grow my own magical beanstalks in paint on the walls of the shed. The bright turquoise walls, giant leaves, and curvy vines give a childlike whimsy to what could have been just another boring storage shed.

SUPPLIES

Latex paint for walls	Template (see page 180)
Roller and paintbrushes	Poster board
Latex paint for leaves	Pencil
Artist's paintbrushes	

1. Paint the walls using a roller. Let the paint dry. Do a second coat if necessary. I used turquoise.

2. Determine how many stems you would like on each wall. My shed is only 8 × 8 feet with 4 windows and a door. I decided upon wavy stems on 3 walls and 2 stems on the wall with the door. I painted them freehand around the shed using dark green.

3. Enlarge the template to the desired size. I wanted the leaves to be giant—mine were 18 inches long.

4. Arrange the leaf template along the side of a stem and trace around it. Continue until the stems are filled. I tilted the leaf at different angles so they would look natural.

5. With an artist's paintbrush, paint the leaves. I used dark green. I did 1 coat of the leaf color so that it would look hand painted. The turquoise background color shows through a bit and adds an interesting texture to the finished wall treatment.

BLOCK-PRINTED LEAF CURTAINS

> PATTERN STYLE: Organic
> PATTERN REPEAT: Straight
> TECHNIQUE: Block Printing

The garden shed doesn't have glass windows—only screens in the openings. It is open to the air all year round. To keep the dust out from our farm and the dirt road we live on, I made some fabric panels that I mounted on the wall with a strip of wood. To continue with the garden theme, I designed a border of flowers and added vertical stripes of leaves. The flower and leaf designs were carved from rubber blocks that I carved with linoleum cutting tools. If you haven't done block printing since art class in grade school, I highly suggest teaching yourself again. After you print your curtains, you can use the blocks for printing tea towels, bags, stationery, and wrapping paper.

SUPPLIES

Templates (see page 180)

Pencil to transfer motif to block before printing

3 × 4-inch Speedball Speedy-Carve block

4 × 5½-inch Speedball Speedy-Carve block

Speedball Lino Cutter linoleum carving tool with 5 cutters

Speedball Fabric Block Printing Ink (see note)

Versatex Screen Printing Ink (see note)

Brayer

Plexiglas for spreading ink

Drop cloth

Curtains to print on

Scrap fabric for testing prints

Auto-fade fabric marker, optional

Soap and water for washing up

NOTE: For this project I tried out 2 different types of ink. I used the Speedball Fabric Block Printing Ink in teal for the leaves and Versatex Screen Printing Ink in fuchsia for the flowers. The Speedball Printing Ink is oil based and yields a print with a hard, crisp edge. The Versatex Screen Printing Ink yields a print with a fuzzy, softer, more antique-feeling edge. Experiment with both kinds and decide which you like best.

1. Photocopy the templates, enlarging them if necessary.

2. Rub the back of the template with a pencil so that the back is covered with graphite. Turn the template over and place it on top of the block with the graphite side facing the block. With a pen or pencil, trace the outlines of the motif. The graphite should transfer to the block.

3. Carve around the lines. Remember: Uncarved areas will print; carved areas will not print. The carving tips are different widths and shapes. Use the larger U-shaped tips to carve away the background. Use the smaller V-shaped tips for the finer details. See more carving instructions on page 125.

4. Spread your drop cloth on a table. Iron the curtain and spread it out on the surface to ready it for printing. Gather the scrap fabric for testing the blocks and lay it flat.

5. Squeeze some ink onto the piece of Plexiglas. If you want to mix a special color, do it now on the glass with a palette knife.

6. Roll the brayer through the ink to spread it. Using the brayer, roll the ink onto the block.

7. With the ink side down, press the block onto the scrap fabric. Look at the design. If you are happy with it, print the motif where desired on the curtain. If you want to carve away more of the block, do it now and make a second test print. Once you are happy with your block, begin printing. I made a horizontal row of 7 flowers along the bottom of the curtain.

I printed 5 vertical rows of leaves above the flower border. To ensure perfect placement, use a yardstick and an auto-fade fabric marker to draw guidelines to follow when printing. To space the motifs evenly along the horizontal border, print 1 motif at the center of the fabric. Print a motif at both the right and left edges of the fabric. Determine how many motifs will fit in the open space. Print them equally spaced across the fabric. If you are fearful, use a ruler and an auto-fade fabric marker to determine and mark exact spots for each print.

8. When finished, clean the block with soap and water so that it can be used again.

9. Allow the ink to dry. Heat-set the ink, following the manufacturer's directions.

BLOUSY ROSE FAUX RUG

PATTERN STYLE: Organic
PATTERN REPEAT: Random
TECHNIQUE: Painting

I wanted the garden shed to be a little room within my garden. With the walls covered with hand-painted leaves, I turned to the floor. It needed a rug, of course. I decided upon a floral "rug" composed of oversized blousy roses edged with graphic borders of bright colors. The roses are very easy to paint—even for someone who has not done much decorative painting. Outlining each of the roses with dark brown makes them stand out from the fuchsia background. I finished the floor with three coats of polyurethane so that it will stand up to weather and foot traffic. This project will take several days to complete in order to let the different layers of color dry between applications.

SUPPLIES

Yardstick	Liner brush
Pencil	Templates (see page 181)
Latex floor paint (I used pink)	Poster board for templates
Latex paint in various colors (see note)	Water-based polyurethane
Paintbrush and roller for solid floor color	
Artist's paintbrushes for roses and borders in various sizes	

NOTE: Since I wanted to use a lot of colors in this "rug," I got tester size jars of latex paint. I used turquoise and lime green for the borders; yellow, pink, orange, and red for the flowers; fuchsia for the background; and dark brown for the outlines.

1. Wash the floor and let it dry.

2. Using a roller and brushes, paint the floor with 2 coats of floor paint, letting each dry between coats.

3. Mark the space for the rug. My rug is 17 inches in from the edge of the floor. With a yardstick, mark the point across 1 side and draw a straight line using the yardstick. Repeat on the remaining 3 sides. Measure 3½ inches in from the first line and draw a second large square inside the first. Repeat and draw a third line. This makes 2 borders and a large open space for the flower design.

4. Enlarge the rose templates to your desired size. My roses measure 6 inches, 8 inches, 12 inches, and 14 inches in diameter.

5. Choose the color for the outside border (I used turquoise). Paint the border and let it dry.

6. Using a template, place it in the center section where desired. Using a pencil, trace around the template. Make the pencil lines loose and curvy—varying the outside shape of each flower. Continue, alternating the different size roses throughout the square. Place some roses so that they are only partly on the rug. The best way to design a random repeat such as this rug is to just begin. Draw 1 rose and then draw the next, leaving space between for the leaves. You can space the roses closely together or farther apart, depending on your taste. Fill in with the smaller rose where needed.

7. Paint the roses using your chosen colors (I used yellow, pink, orange, and red). Paint

a circle in the middle of each rose for the center. Continue until all roses and centers are painted. If necessary, apply a second coat.

8. Paint the background behind the roses. To choose my color, I tried out several by testing them in small sections to see which I liked best. I chose fuchsia. Apply a second coat if necessary.

9. Outline the flowers with a liner brush and a dark color (I used dark brown).

10. Paint the inner border. I did this last so that I could chose a color that would coordinate with all the elements of the faux rug—the border, the background, and the flowers (I used lime green).

11. Apply polyurethane with a brush. I applied 3 coats over the entire floor, letting it dry a day in between each coat.

CHAPTER FIVE

IN THE ORCHARD AND UNDER THE PERGOLA

WE ARE SO LUCKY TO LIVE WHERE THERE ARE FOUR SEASONS TO EVERY YEAR. IN THE SPRING AFTER LONG COLD WINTERS, I CRAVE THE OUTDOORS. EVERY DAY—SPRING, SUMMER, AND FALL—I SPEND HOURS AND HOURS OUTSIDE IN MY GARDEN, TAKING WALKS AND ENJOYING the sunshine. One of my favorite things to do is eat outdoors. Food just tastes so much better when served in the fresh air under the trees.

I love to bring the outside into our home by decorating with vases of flowers, but truthfully, it is even more special to bring the inside out. Packing up a picnic basket with lunch and walking down into the orchard slows down the day and gives an opportunity to really enjoy nature. Spreading a hand-printed tablecloth out on the ground and spending an hour or two forgetting about real life is such an indescribable luxury. Enjoying snacks and a glass of wine under the pergola eases tensions and is a perfect way to wind down and relax.

UPCYCLED VINTAGE PICNIC BASKET

> **PATTERN STYLE:** Organic
> **PATTERN REPEAT:** Random
> **TECHNIQUE:** Painting

A picnic basket conjures up memories of fun outdoor adventures to new places, hours spent walking through the woods, discovering berries, rocks, and lichen, clambering across streams, and telling stories. Inside the basket, plates, utensils, and delicious food guarantee a yummy meal even if the bugs won't be far behind.

Many a picnic basket can be found at yard sales and flea markets. I found this one and started dreaming about the picnic I would use it for in our apple orchard. When I got it home, I spray painted it to give it a new lease on life. On the top, I painted a pattern of flowers to add to the old-fashioned charm.

SUPPLIES

Picnic basket

Spray paint (I used green)

Drop cloth

Latex paint (I used red, yellow, and brown)

Artist's brushes in various sizes

Liner brush in size 0

Template (see page 182)

Tape

Poster board

Pencil

1. Wash the picnic basket with soap and water and let it dry thoroughly.

2. Working outside or in a well-ventilated area, spread the drop cloth on the ground or a table. Spray the basket with the spray paint. I did 2 coats, letting it dry overnight between coats. Use short quick bursts of paint to alleviate drips.

3. Photocopy the flower template and cut it out. Tape the motif to the poster board and cut it out.

4. Randomly place the motif on the lid of the basket and trace around it with a pencil. Position the flowers with varying amounts of space between. Place some of the flowers part way off the sides of the basket.

5. Using latex paint, fill in the flowers with your chosen color. I used red. Let it dry and apply a second coat if necessary.

6. Using latex paint, paint a small circle for the center of each flower. I used yellow.

7. Using the liner brush, outline each flower. I used dark brown. Let the paint dry.

BLOCK-PRINTED BASIL LEAF NAPKINS

PATTERN STYLE: Organic
PATTERN REPEAT: Straight
TECHNIQUE: Block Printing

In the south of France, carved wooden blocks have been used since 1664 to print colorful fabrics full of floral patterns. Originally inspired by fabrics imported from India, the design of the French fabrics began to morph into something now known as Provencal designs. Many of these fabrics feature floral stripes and borders. Although my hand-cut block is much simpler than its Provencal inspiration, it gives a similar look to these fringed napkins.

Table linens are the perfect project to try out new printing techniques. They are quick to print and make beautiful gifts. I designed this linoleum block design to be used as a border around the four sides of a napkin. I began the block design with a basil leaf from my garden. I quickly sketched its shape and veins. By placing the sketch in the four corners of my block, I had a design that would look good as a border. I connected the leaves in my sketch with stems that crossed each other to form an × shape. When deciding how to stamp a design, I practiced on scraps of fabric. At first I printed an overall design using a straight repeat. I quickly decided that the crossed leaf design would be stronger as a border element. Designing handmade prints is trial and error. The experimentation stage is often the most fun part of the process for me.

SUPPLIES

- Finished napkins (see "Basic Technique: Making Napkins" on page 37 for how to make your own)
- Template (see page 183)
- Pencil
- 3 × 4-inch Speedball Speedy-Carve block
- Speedball Lino Cutter linoleum carving tool with 5 cutters
- Speedball Fabric Block Printing Ink (I used green)
- Brayer
- Plexiglas for spreading ink
- Drop cloth
- Scrap fabric for testing prints
- Quilting ruler
- Auto-fade fabric marker

1. Photocopy the template. Rub the back of the template with a pencil so that the back is covered with graphite. Turn the template over and place it on top of the block with the graphite side facing the block. With a pen or pencil, trace the outlines of the motif. The graphite should transfer to the block.

2. Carve around the lines. Remember: Uncarved areas will print; carved areas will not print. Before printing on your napkins, do a test print on a piece of scrap fabric. If it is satisfactory, begin printing. If you want to carve more to clean up around the motif or to make the details more prominent, wash the block, dry it, and recarve. Continue testing and carving until you are happy with your printing block.

3. Spread the drop cloth on a table. Iron the napkins to prepare them for printing. Spread one out on the surface.

4. Squeeze some ink onto the Plexiglas. If you want to mix a special color, do it now with a palette knife.

5. Roll the brayer through the ink to spread it. Using the brayer, roll the ink onto the carved block.

6. With the ink side down, press the block onto the test fabric. Do a few more test prints to get the feel of the pressure needed. For good transfer, press hard over the entire block and give it a hard tap to help the transfer of the ink.

7. Mark the borders for placement. Using a ruler and auto-fade fabric marker, draw a line 1 inch in from the edge of the napkin. Mark the center point on each of the 4 sides. Begin printing by positioning the first print at the center point of the first border. Next, place prints at the right and left corners of the napkins. Place the next 2 prints in the open space between the center and edge prints. Repeat on the 3 remaining sides. You should have 5 motifs at each edge of the napkin.

8. When you are finished, clean the block with soap and water so that it can be used again.

9. Allow the ink to dry. Heat-set the ink following the manufacturer's directions.

LINEN TABLECLOTH WITH PRINTED LEAVES

PATTERN STYLE: Organic
PATTERN REPEAT: Random
TECHNIQUE: Stamping

Raw linen has been used for utilitarian textiles for hundreds of years. When spun and woven, the raw flax fiber that linen is made from has a beautiful slubby texture and an earthy, natural color. This practical fabric was the perfect base for a tablecloth I printed with leaves using translucent textile paint. I made the stamps for printing by tracing leaves I found outdoors. You can use the templates I have provided but, better yet, take an adventure and pick up different shapes of leaves to become inspiration for your very own stamps for printing.

SUPPLIES

FOR THE STAMPS

Templates
(see pages 184–85)

Craft foam with adhesive backing

1-inch-thick foam building insulation

Scissors

Tape

Utility knife

FOR THE TABLECLOTH

Linen fabric in natural color (mine measured 48 by 72 inches)

Sewing machine

Steam iron

Drop cloth

Jacquard Textile Color in 3 shades:

116 Apple Green

117 Emerald Green

118 Olive Green

Versatex Fixer, optional

½-inch and 1-inch foam brushes

Deli containers with lids

Large table for printing

Fabric and craft scissors

1. Prewash your fabric and hang it to dry.

2. To fringe the ends, sew a straight line of machine stitching approximately ½ inch in from each end of the fabric. Using a needle, unweave the threads horizontal to the selvedge until you have reached the stitching. If the thread is caught in the stitching in the middle of the tablecloth, trim it off next to the stitching.

3. Following the instructions, assemble the foam stamps (see "Basic Technique: Making Stamps" on page 33).

4. Cover a large table with a canvas drop cloth to become a printing surface.

5. Iron the fabric and lay it on the printing surface.

153

6. Add the Versatex Fixer to the paint (optional).

7. Begin with the borders. Use all 3 colors of paint randomly. Follow the basic printing instructions for printing with foam stamps (see "Stamping Tips" on page 32). Using the smallest leaf, stamp all 4 edges of the cloth with leaves that are placed diagonally along the edge of the cloth, approximately ½ to 1 inch in from each edge. Each leaf should rotate 180 degrees from the stamp closest to it.

8. Beginning with the largest leaf, randomly stamp 6 leaves in different sections of the cloth using the color of your choice. Repeat with the 4 other stamps. The cloth should have an open feeling with large areas of open space between each stamp.

9. Heat-set the paint, following manufacturer's directions.

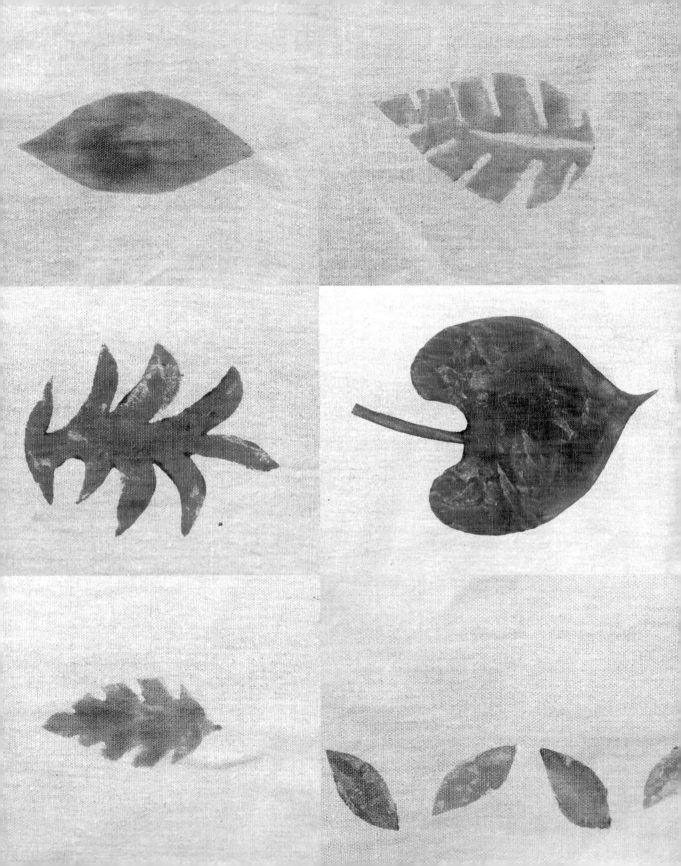

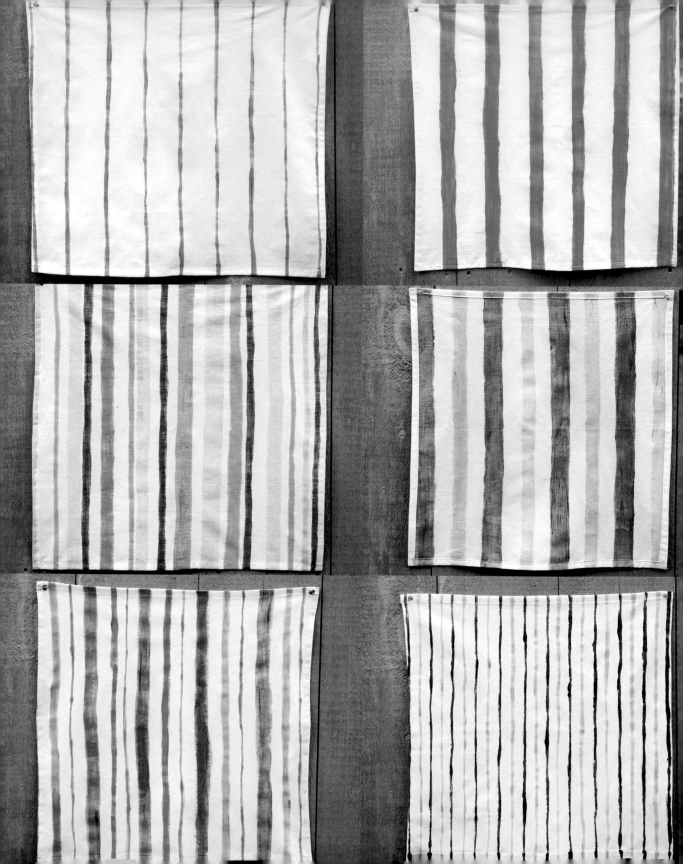

PAINTED STRIPE NAPKINS

PATTERN STYLE: Geometric
PATTERN REPEAT:
Both Straight and Random
TECHNIQUE: Painting

Stripes have been a classic motif in textiles for thousands of years. They never look old—in fact they always look modern. When just beginning to learn to paint on fabric, stripes are a good design motif to use. Besides learning about spacing and pattern repeats, you will also get the feel for the paint and how the brush reacts to the fabric you are painting on.

Hand-painted stripes add a lovely handmade quality to any project you make. The unevenness of the paint cover, the irregular-width lines, and the often not-perfectly-straight lines are endearing. I chose shades of blues and greens and had fun experimenting with the different color combinations and stripe sizes. The bright white fabric made the colors stand out. Once you make one set of napkins, experiment with other colors or even painting stripes on colored fabrics.

SUPPLIES

Cotton or linen napkins (see "Basic Technique: Making Napkins" on page 37 for how to make your own)

Drop cloth

Various sizes flat and round artist's brushes, from ¼ inch to ¾ inch

Jacquard Textile Color fabric paint in assorted colors (I used various shades of blue and green)

Jacquard Textile Color #100 Colorless Extender

Versatex Fixer, optional

Deli containers

Steam iron

1. Cover your work surface with a drop cloth.

2. Mix the paint colors in the deli containers using the colorless extender to lighten. I used shades of green, chartreuse, turquoise, lupine blue, and ultramarine blue.

3. Add the Versatex Fixer (optional).

4. Using a steady hand, paint stripes on each napkin. Don't worry if they are not perfectly straight or perfectly spaced—they are supposed to look handmade, not mass produced. Make different stripe patterns with lines of varying thickness—from ¼ inch to 2 inches thick. Begin at 1 side of the napkin and paint stripes across the entire surface, working either from left to right or right to left.

5. If you are not using the Versatex Fixer, follow the manufacturer's directions to heat-set the fabric paint. Iron to neaten.

STENCILED SERVING TRAY

PATTERN STYLE: Geometric
PATTERN REPEAT: Straight
TECHNIQUE:
Painting and Stenciling

There are many treasures to be found at yard sales and thrift stores if you are a crafty soul. An object that someone else discarded can often be picked up inexpensively and transformed into something fabulous using paint and a little imagination. That's how this tray project began—a slightly rusted tin tray just waiting for its next life.

For this project, I used stencil film with removable adhesive backing to make the plaid design. After cutting the squares, I applied them to the tray diagonally with equal spacing all around. After stenciling the plaid lines, I outlined the plaid lines freehand using metallic gold paint. I added details to the shaped edge of my tray. Depending on the shape of your tray, you may have to improvise your border treatment. What began as someone else's trash is now my treasure.

SUPPLIES

Steel wool

Rustoleum Spray Rust Reformer

Adhesive stencil film with grid outline on back (I used Martha Stewart brand)

Scissors

Spray paint in chosen color (I used Rustoleum turquoise)

Enamel paint for plaid lines (I used Rustoleum black)

Enamel metallic paint (I used Testor's gold and blue)

1-inch foam brush

Detail liner brush

Paint thinner for brush cleanup

1. If your tray has a bit of rust, wash it and remove any very loose rust with steel wool. Working outside or in a well-ventilated area, spray both sides of the tray with Rust Reformer, letting it dry as instructed by the manufacturer.

2. Using your chosen color of spray paint, spray 2 even coats on each side of the tray. I used turquoise.

3. Cut out 2-inch squares from the stencil adhesive film using the grid lines on the back as guides.

4. Determine the center of the tray. Remove the paper backing from a square and carefully place it, sticky side down, diagonally in the center of the tray. Build the pattern around this center square by placing the remainder of the squares around the center square. Leave approximately ¼ inch between each square to form the grid pattern. The stencil film is very forgiving, and it can be removed and placed down again and again. Eyeball the spacing and correct it if necessary.

5. Continue placing squares until the entire tray is full. At the edge, the squares will lap over the border. When you are happy with the spacing, press firmly around all the edges so the paint will not seep under the stencil film.

6. Using the foam brush, paint the spaces between the squares using an up and down pouncing motion. Let the paint dry. When the paint is completely dry, remove the stencil squares.

7. Using blue enamel paint and the liner brush, paint the rim of the tray following the photo. I painted 2 borders. Between them, I painted slightly curved vertical lines. Let the paint dry.

8. Using the detail liner brush and gold enamel, paint around each square. Paint large polka dots along the outer rim. Let the paint dry.

IN THE ORCHARD AND UNDER THE PERGOLA

REFURBISHED METAL TABLETOP

PATTERN STYLE: Organic
PATTERN REPEAT: Random
TECHNIQUE: Painting

I had this round table made by a roofing contractor almost twenty years ago. It was made by wrapping a large sheet of metal around a large plywood circle. It sits on a base made from a vintage European washtub with pretty vertical embossed lines that I found at the Brimfield Flea Market. The tabletop had begun to rust. I discovered Rust Reformer in the spray paint aisle of the hardware store and went to work hiding the rust. For the design, I channeled Henri Matisse and made organic shapes from cut-out paper—the same kind he made at the end of his long and prolific career. The large leaf shapes are a bold graphic statement that looks like a tablecloth.

SUPPLIES

Rusted metal tabletop

Steel wool

Rustoleum Rust Reformer Spray

Scissors

Spray paint in chosen color (I used Rustoleum green)

Enamel oil paint for leaves (I used Rustoleum black)

Poster board

Pencil

Artist's paintbrush in round size 8

Paint thinner for brush cleanup

1. Wash the table, removing any loose rust bits with steel wool. Working outside or in a well-ventilated area, spray the tabletop with Rust Reformer, letting it dry as instructed by the manufacturer.

2. Using your chosen color of spray paint, spray 2 even coats, following the manufacturer's directions.

3. Make your own stem and leaf templates. From poster board, cut 5 long, curved stems in various lengths that are about 1½ inches wide. They should fit the shape of the table. Cut a couple of different-sized leaf shapes from the poster board.

4. Place the stem templates randomly on the tabletop and trace around them. Add leaves to each stem by placing the leaf templates at different angles on both sides of the stem. Trace around the templates. The leaves should look natural and uneven, as if they are being found on the forest floor.

5. Using enamel paint and an artist's paintbrush, fill in the stems and leaves with paint. Let the paint dry. Do a second coat if necessary.

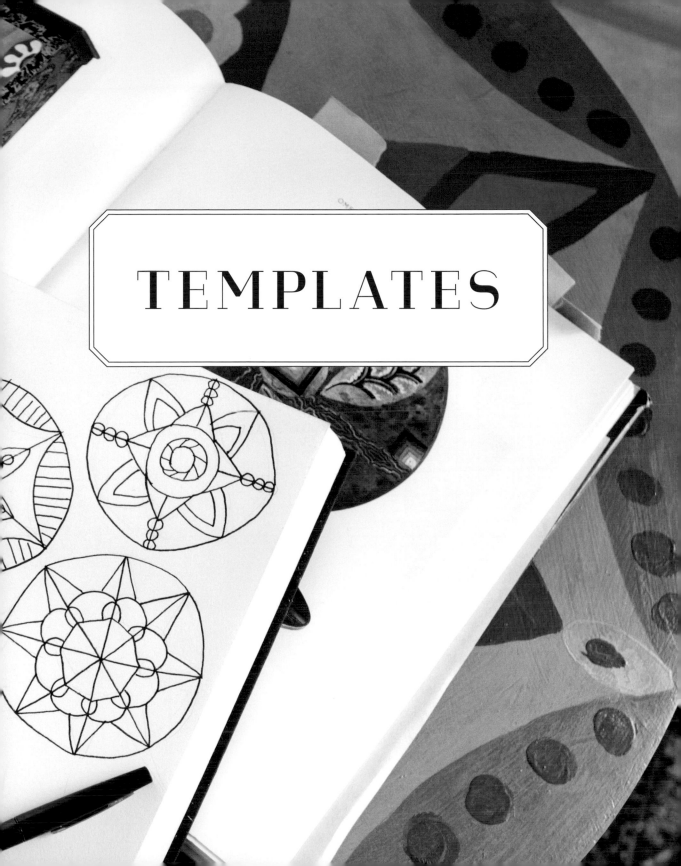

TEMPLATES

GEOMETRIC STRIPED TABLECLOTH
AND ALL-OVER GEOMETRIC NAPKINS

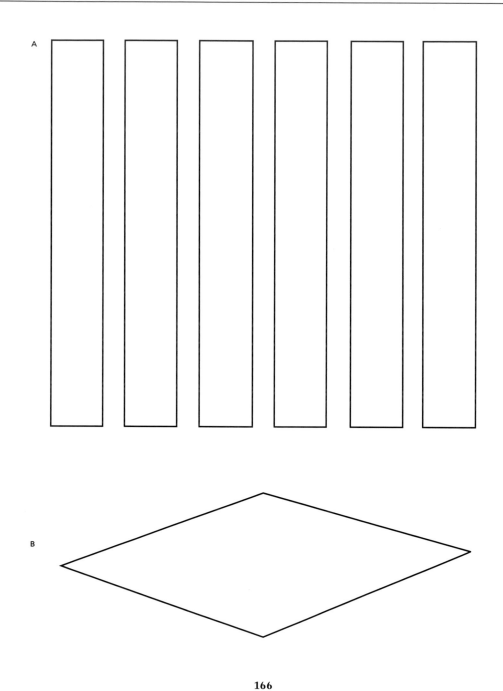

A

B

C

D

E

F

G

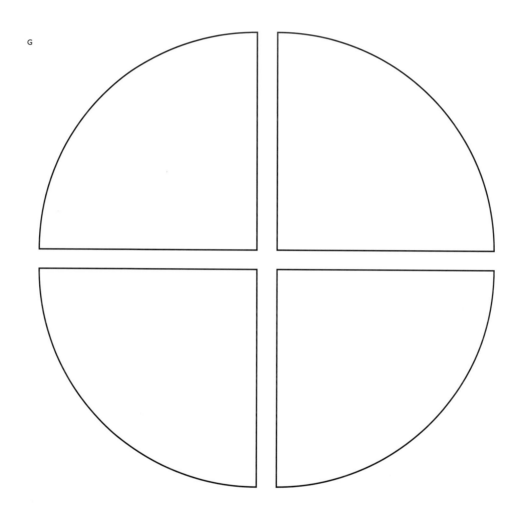

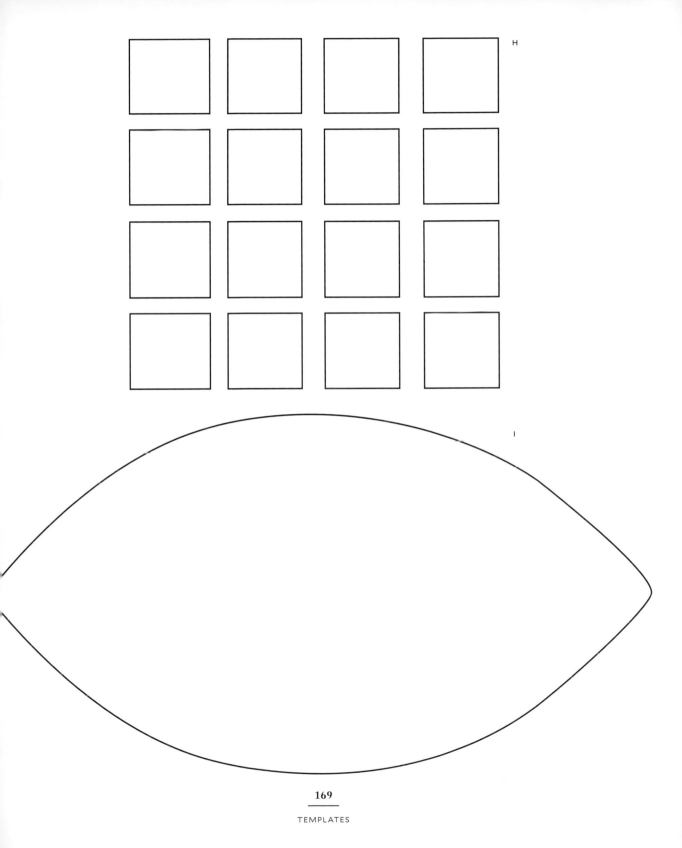

H

I

TEMPLATES

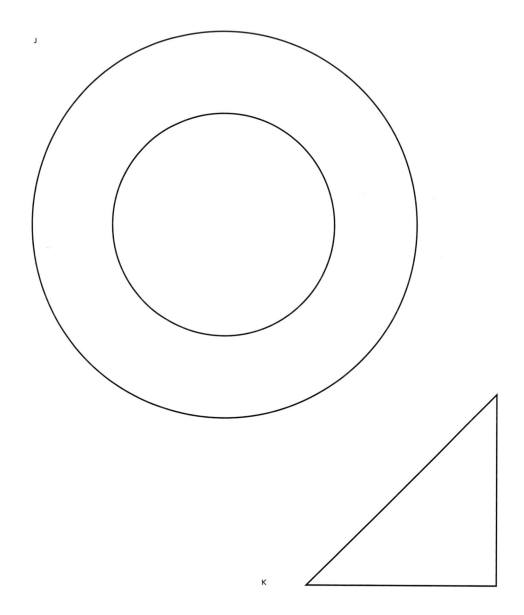

J

K

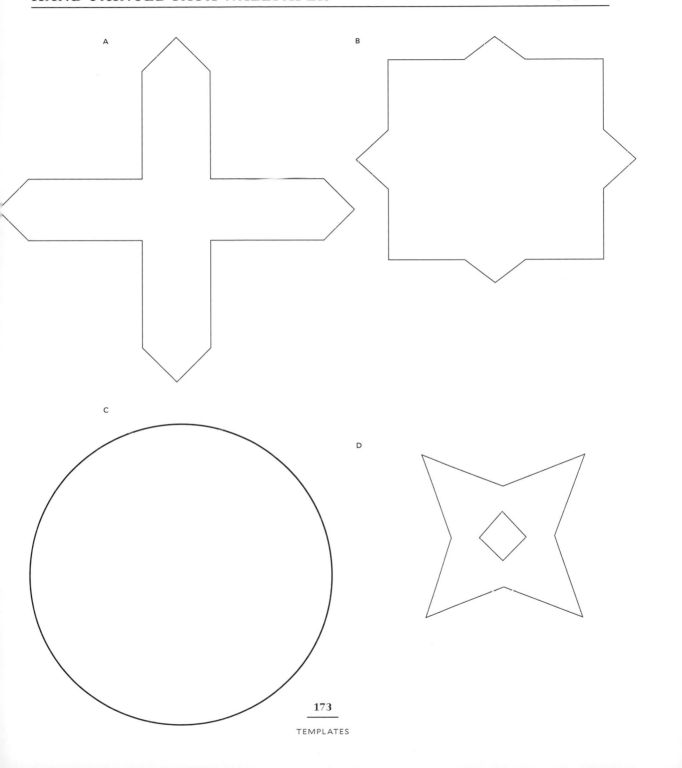

A

B

C

D

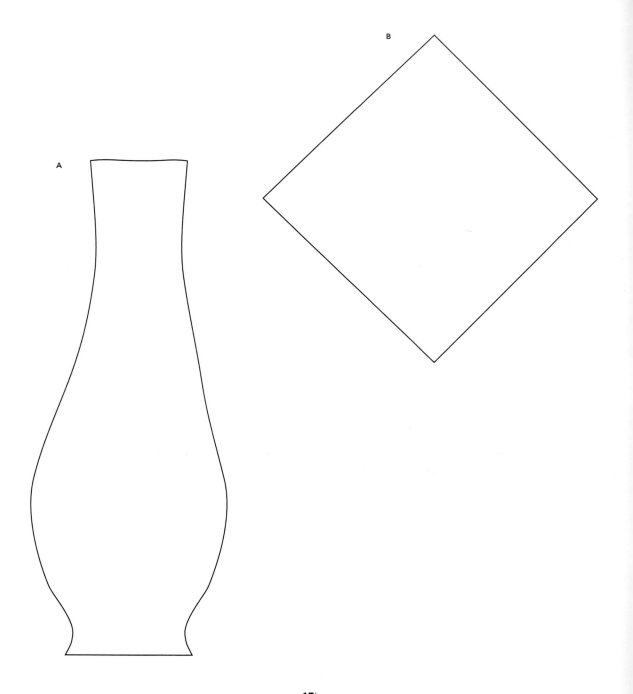

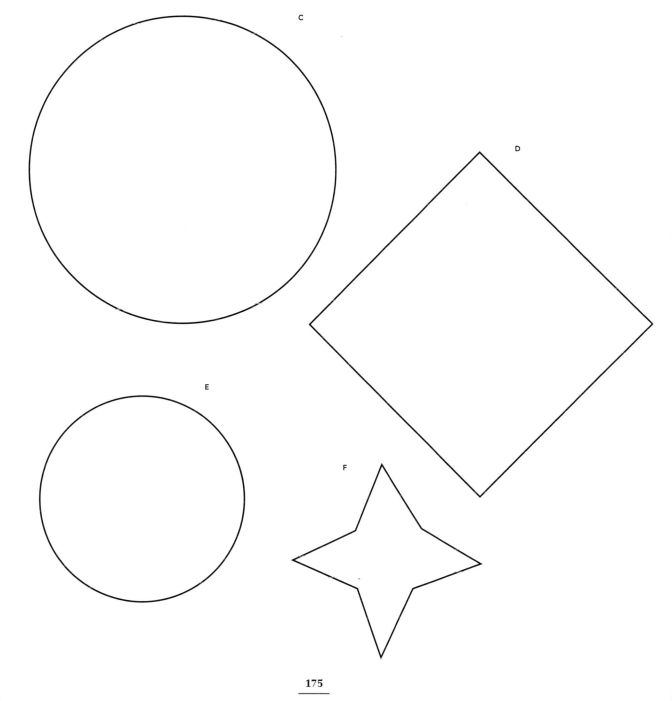

C

D

E

F

COMBED STOOL

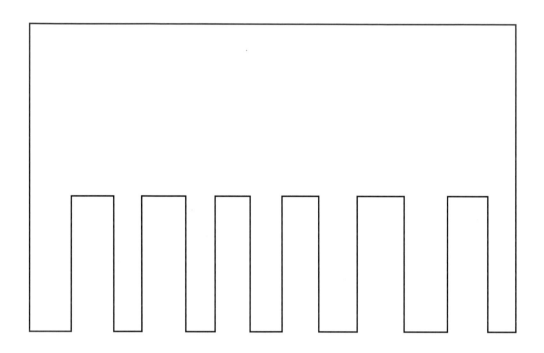

DOTS AND SPOTS PILLOW

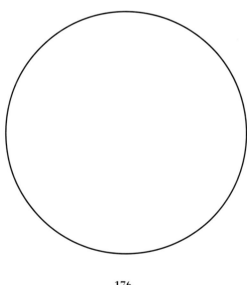

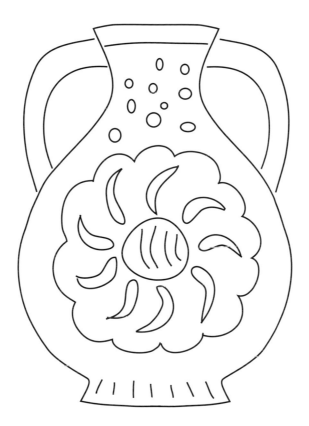

JACK AND THE BEANSTALK FAUX WALLPAPER

Enlarge by 400%

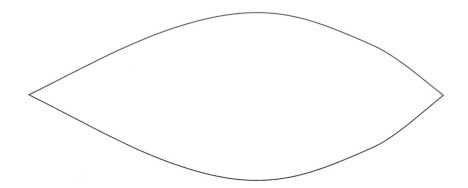

BLOCK-PRINTED LEAF CURTAINS

Shown at full size

BLOUSY ROSE FAUX RUG

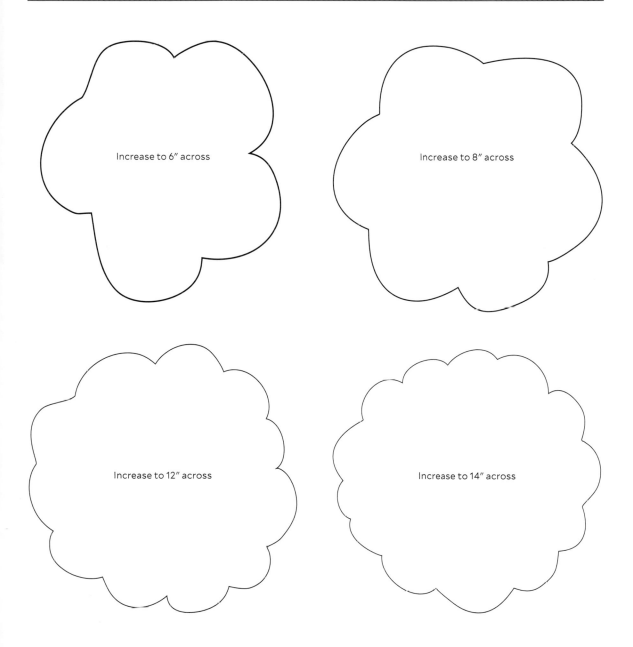

Increase to 6" across

Increase to 8" across

Increase to 12" across

Increase to 14" across

RESOURCES

BOOKS

This is a list of some of my favorite books from my library. Many of the authors have written multiple books, and I urge you to look for all of their titles.

Block Print: Everything You Need to Know for Printing with Lino Blocks, Rubber Blocks, Foam Sheets, and Stamp Sets by Andrea Lauren

Charleston: A Bloomsbury House and Garden by Quentin Bell

Costume Patterns and Designs by Max Tilke

Dreaming in Color by Kaffe Fassett (or any of his books)

Dufy by Dora Perez-Tibi

A Field Guide to Fabric Design: Design, Print & Sell Your Own Fabric by Kim Kight

The Illuminated Life of Maud Lewis by Lance Woolaver

Mastering the Art of Fabric Printing and Design by Laurie Wisburn

Matisse the Master: A Life of Henri Matisse—The Conquest of Colour by Hilary Spurling

Paint Magic by Jocasta Innes (or any of her books)

Print Workshop: Hand-Printing Techniques and Truly Original Projects by Christine Schmidt

Russian Textiles: Printed Cloth for the Bazaars of Central Asia by Susan Meller

Textiles of the Islamic World by John Gillow

Tricia Guild's Country Color by Tricia Guild (or any of her books)

The Unknown Matisse: A Life of Henri Matisse: The Early Years by Hilary Spurling

World Textiles by John Gillow

CRAFT SUPPLIES

DHARMA TRADING COMPANY—
www.dharmatrading.com
(for textile paints and fabrics)

DICK BLICK—
www.dickblick.com
(for art supplies)

KRISTIN NICHOLAS DESIGNS—
www.kristinnicholas.com
(for linen fabrics and crewel
embroidery threads)

SPOONFLOWER—
www.spoonflower.com
(for digital printing on demand)

ACKNOWLEDGMENTS

When I look back on this book project, it occurs to me that so many people have helped me write and create it. There are some folks who I remember specifically and want to name here but there are so many friends, teachers, and authors who have taught and shared with me. I want to thank all of the people who have shared their skills and knowledge with me in the past and that I now have the good fortune to share with you. I pass on my knowledge in the spirit that you too will share what you learn from my book with your friends. After all, what is knowledge if it isn't shared?

Thanks so much to my teachers who helped me continue to be curious and keep learning. Robin Cashen taught me to sew a dress when I was nine years old. Dorothy Airola taught me couture dressmaking at Dover High School in northern New Jersey. My immigrant grandmother, Frieda Nicholas, taught me to crochet, quilt, and embroider. My mom, Nancy Nicholas, taught me the importance of home and family and so much more. My fiber art professor, Vera Kaminski, taught me about the world of fiber art and expanded my ideas on what the needle arts could be. My textile professor, Jan Else, taught me about the incredible anthropological and decorative world of world textiles. My friends Yola Shashaty, George Singeley, and Sally Lee suggested that I sit down with them and paint a fish one weekend on an island in Maine. I will be forever grateful in the confidence they had in my undiscovered ability to paint and their push for me to expand my skills beyond the needlework world. My sisters Lynn, Laurie, Nancy, and Jennifer have been with me my entire life and have shared in the creative chaos that is life and art.

I had some help with the projects in this book. My friend Kevin Gray helped me with several of the projects that needed power tools. My nephew Nicholas Duprey helped me clean out the sheds so they could be made anew. Bonnie Reardon made the crochet afghan. Kim and Bill Chagnon upholstered the paisley chair and slip-covered the kitchen wing chair.

Thank you, Rikki Snyder, for your fantastic eye and photographs. You turn my visual dreams into beautiful images and you are so much fun to spend time with. Thanks to my friend Gail Callahan for your incredible help during the photo shoots. My literary agent, Linda Roghaar, continues to have faith in my ability to put a project like this together. Thank you to Linda and to the fine folks at Roost Books, including editor extraordinaire Jenn Urban-Brown, Breanna Locke, Daniel Urban-Brown, and Shubhani Sarkar. You have all made this book come together so beautifully. Thanks to the creative sales and publicity team at Roost, including Jess Townsend and Claire Kelly.

Thank you to my friends Cathy Payson, Candi Jensen, Linda Pratt, Sally Lee, Kay Dougherty,

and Debbie Herron for keeping my spirits up as deadlines loomed. Thanks to the many readers of my blog *Getting Stitched on the Farm* for your support of my creative and farming life.

And lastly to my husband, Mark Duprey, and daughter, Julia Nicholas Duprey—thank you for the patience, love, and support you both show as we all lived through the year of creativity, confusion, and chaos as this book came to life.

ABOUT THE AUTHOR

KRISTIN NICHOLAS is an all-around creative artist who works with paint, yarn, thread, fabric, clay, and more. Throughout her work, her love of color and pattern is the cohesive element that gives the definitive style to her interior decoration, paintings, ceramics, and needlework. Kristin is an avid gardener and her love of flowers and nature inspires much of her work. Her family's 1751 farmhouse has been the canvas for her creative forays for the past twenty years.

Kristin was the creative director of a yarn company for sixteen years. She has appeared on PBS's *Knit and Crochet Now!* for many seasons and has appeared on *Martha Stewart TV* and many DIY television shows. She teaches various subjects online on the Creativebug and Craftsy platforms. She is the author of numerous books, including *Colorful Stitchery* and *Crafting a Colorful Home* (Roost Books).

Kristin lives on Leyden Glen Farm, a working sheep farm in Western Massachusetts, with her husband Mark and daughter Julia. Together they raise grass-fed lambs to feed the local community. On her blog *Getting Stitched on the Farm* she shares their colorful lives on the farm. You can see more of her work on her website www.kristinnicholas.com.

Muhu naine (1920. a. paiku) — (tahvel XXXII) 1) Suuri tikand. 2) Suka tikand. 3) Tanu tikand ja lôikeskeem. 4) Seeliku tikitud pook. 5) Seeliku triibustik. **Jämaja naine** (leinarôivastus) — (tahvel XXVIII). 6) Seeliku allääre kaunistused. 7) Vöö kiri. **Kihelkonna naine** (tahvel XXX). 8) Lahttasku skeem. 9) Seeliku triibustik. 10) Vöö kiri.

Kihelkonna mees (tahvel XXX) 11) Seelikureaaela skeem. 12) Võrkvöö skeem. **Kihelkonna laps** (tahvel XXX). 13) Seeliku triibustik. 14) Seelikutraksiche kiri. Vöö kiri. **Anseküla neiu ja naine** (tahvel XXVIII). 16) Liistiku koekiri. 17) Vöö kiri. 18) Seeliku triibustik ja allääre pook.